The W[...] the Gospels

Missionaries of God's Love

The Women of the Gospels

Missionaries of God's Love

Mary Ann Getty-Sullivan

The Word Among Us Press
7115 Guilford Drive, Suite 100
Frederick, Maryland 21704
wau.org

ISBN: 978-1-59325-170-3

21 20 19 18 17   5 6 7 8 9

Nihil Obstat: The Rev. Michael Morgan, Chancellor
                Censor Librorum
                May 11, 2010

Imprimatur: +Most Rev. Victor Galeone
                Bishop of St. Augustine
                May 11, 2010

Unless otherwise noted, Scripture passages contained herein are from the New Revised Standard Version Bible: Catholic Edition, copyright © 1989, 1993, Division of Christian Education of the National Council of the Churches of Christ in the United States. All rights reserved. Used with permission.

Excerpts from the English translation of the *Catechism of the Catholic Church* for use in the United States of America, copyright ©1994, United States Catholic Conference, Inc.—Libreria Editrice Vaticana. Used with permission.

Cover and text design by David Crosson
Cover art: Etienne Parrocel, (1696-1776)
Christ and the Samaratin Woman. Photo: Gérard Blot
Musee Fesch, Ajaccio, Corsica, Corsica, France
Photo Credit: Réunion des Musées Nationaux/Art Resource, NY

Made and printed in the United States of America

Library of Congress Control Number: 2010925977

Contents

Welcome to
The Word Among Us
Keys to the Bible

Have you ever lost your keys? Everyone seems to have at least one "lost keys" story to tell. Maybe you had to break a window of your house or wait for the auto club to let you into your car. Whatever you had to do probably cost you—in time, energy, money, or all three. Keys are definitely important items to have on hand!

The guides in The Word Among Us Keys to the Bible series are meant to provide you with a handy set of keys that can "unlock" the treasures of the Scriptures for you. Scripture is God's living word. Within its pages we meet the Lord. So as we study and meditate on Scripture and unlock its many treasures, we discover the riches it contains—and in the process, we grow in intimacy with God.

Since 1982 *The Word Among Us* magazine has helped Catholics develop a deeper relationship with the Lord through daily meditations that bring the Scriptures to life. More than ever, Catholics today desire to read and pray with the Scriptures, and many have begun to form small faith-sharing groups to explore the Bible together.

We designed the Keys to the Bible series after conducting a survey among our magazine readers to learn what they wanted in a Catholic Bible study. We found that they were looking for easy-to-understand, faith-filled materials that approach Scripture from a clearly Catholic perspective. Moreover, they wanted a Bible study that shows them how they can apply what they learn from Scripture to their everyday lives. They also asked for sessions that they could complete in an hour or two.

Our goal was to design a simple, easy-to-use Bible study guide that is also challenging and thought provoking. We hope that this guide fulfills those admittedly ambitious goals. We are confident, however, that taking the time to go through this guide—whether by yourself, with a friend, or in a small group—will be a worthwhile endeavor that will bear fruit in your life.

How to Use the Guides in This Series

The study guides in the Keys to the Bible series are divided into six sessions that each deal with a particular aspect of the topic. Before starting the first session, take the time to read the introduction, which sets the stage for the sessions that follow.

Whether you use this guide for personal reflection and study, as part of a faith-sharing group, or as an aid in your prayer time, be sure to begin each session with prayer. Ask God to open his word to you and to speak to you personally. Read each Scripture passage slowly and carefully. Then take as much time as you need to meditate on the passage and pursue any thoughts it brings to mind. When you are ready, move on to the accompanying commentary, which offers various insights into the text.

Two sets of questions are included in each session to help you "mine" the Scripture passage and discover its relevance to your life. Those under the heading "Understand!" focus on the text itself and help you grasp what it means. Occasionally a question allows for a variety of answers and is meant to help you explore the passage from several angles. "Grow!" questions are intended to elicit a personal response by helping you examine your life in light of the values and truths that you uncover through your study of the Scripture passage and its setting. Under the headings "Reflect!" and "Act!" we offer suggestions to help you respond concretely to the challenges posed by the passage.

Finally, pertinent quotations from the Fathers of the Church as well as insights from contemporary writers appear throughout each session. Coupled with relevant selections from the *Catechism of the Catholic Church* and information about the history, geography, and culture of first-century Palestine, these selections (called "In the Spotlight") add new layers of understanding and insight to your study.

As is true with any learning resource, you will benefit the most from this study by writing your answers to the questions in the spaces provided. The simple act of writing can help you formulate your thoughts more clearly—and will also give you a record of your reflections and spiritual growth that you can return to in the future to see how much God has accomplished in your life. End your reading or study with a prayer thanking God for what you have learned—and ask the Holy Spirit to guide you in living out the call you have been given as a Christian in the world today.

Although the Scripture passages to be studied and the related verses for your reflection are printed in full in each guide (from the New Revised Standard Version: Catholic Edition), you will find it helpful to have a Bible on hand for looking up other passages and cross-references or for comparing different translations.

The format of the guides in The Word Among Us Keys to the Bible series is especially well suited for use in small groups. Some recommendations and practical tips for using this guide in a Bible discussion group are offered on pages 112–115.

We hope that this guide will unlock the meaning of the Scriptures for you. As you accompany these women on their journey of discipleship, may the Holy Spirit draw you closer to the heavenly Father, increase your love for him, and deepen your desire to follow Jesus as they did.

The Word Among Us Press

Introduction
Women and Discipleship

The positive images of women found in both the Old and New Testaments are intriguing, especially because they cannot be explained in the light of the dominant patriarchal culture that produced them. Indeed, they are contrary to most of what we know about the time period and its culture and values.

The gospels illustrate this point very well. Despite almost certainly being written by men, the gospels portray women as significant and influential members of Jesus' entourage as he proceeds from his home in Galilee to his death in Jerusalem. As Jesus makes his way to Jerusalem and the cross, many men and women are attracted to him because of his miracles and his teachings. As they begin to understand sacrifice and suffering as intrinsically involved in following a crucified Messiah, fear, disappointment, and other weaknesses cause some to lose faith, and many fall by the wayside. But some women, as well as some men, persevere even through the crucifixion and beyond to the resurrection. These followers become missionaries who continue to spread the message that Jesus had entrusted to them when he said, "Go therefore and make disciples of all nations" (Matthew 28:19).

The gospels in particular paint a vision of equality of men and women, made in the image of God, that is presented as characteristic of the kingdom of God that Jesus came to inaugurate among us. Jesus performs miracles for foreign mothers of daughters as well as for prominent leaders on behalf of their sons. Jesus speaks in parables using women's experiences of baking bread and sweeping floors as well as the experiences of men who rule kingdoms or entrust extravagant sums of money to servants while they travel the world. Jesus' teachings and example are inclusive and convey a dignity for both women and men.

Both men and women are challenged as much today as they were in Jesus' time by his message, which calls for a change of heart. Men and women alike are invited by Jesus to convert their lives to reflect the radical differences between business as usual in a world driven by competition for power, money, and prestige, and the values of mercy, justice, and peace that are characteristic of the kingdom of God. In this sense, interpreting the gospels is a very dynamic and open-ended process indeed. We are constantly discovering and learning new ways that we can make the gospels relevant in our own lives. Especially in view of contemporary interest in the Scriptures and the more accessible methods of interpreting them, we are compelled as believers to accept their challenges and their invitation to become more authentically the People of God.

A Portrait of Discipleship

Our interest in women in the gospels comes with a caveat: the New Testament does not include such a category or theme. Our questions are not the questions that the Evangelists wondered about, since the gospels are not necessarily about women but about discipleship. It is also important to remember that the people described in the gospels have more than historical importance for us; they have symbolic and theological significance.

There is no single formula for or simple definition of discipleship in the gospels. Rather, discipleship is described in flesh-and-blood terms in the gospels' stories, featuring people with traits we can identify with and learn from. Fear and doubt, the envy of the leaders, and the confusion and misunderstanding of some of Jesus' followers prevented them from wholeheartedly embracing the message that the kingdom of God had arrived. But those who were truly poor and open, hungry for justice, and intent on being healed by Jesus responded positively when he asked, "What do you want me to do for you?" (Mark 10:51). And women as well as men fit the description of true disciples of Jesus, as evidenced by their response to him and his message.

While it cannot be said that the gospels deliberately treat "women" as a theme, it is remarkable that no woman encounters Jesus and goes away unchanged or unconverted. Every woman who is said to have met up with Jesus responds with faith and is portrayed positively.

The gospels present various descriptions of the disciples of Jesus, but all would agree that a disciple (the word means "learner") is someone who is attracted to Jesus by a call and follows him, and who continues to learn his teachings even as he and they progress on the journey to the cross. For example, Mark says that Jesus appointed the Twelve "to be with him, and to be sent out to proclaim the message" (Mark 3:14). Luke has Jesus saying that his disciples are "those who have stood by me in my trials" (Luke 22:28) and are "the witnesses of these things"—his death and resurrection (24:48). John says that the disciples are those who come to Jesus, believe in him, and remain with him (1:39; 15:1).

The fact that women are portrayed in such a consistently positive way in the gospels seems to be essential to the revelation of the kingdom of God. Whereas in this world women are often among the disenfranchised, the neglected, and the forgotten, the kingdom that Jesus inaugurates offers a very different valuation of them. And this difference is part of the message he commands his followers to preach by word and example.

At times the gospels actually seem to paint a rather harsh or even negative portrait of the disciples. For example, Mark implies that the disciples did not understand Jesus and were very slow to believe (8:17). Despite seeing many miracles, they were hesitant and doubtful. They asked each other, "Who then is this?" (4:41). Even when Jesus predicted his own death in Jerusalem, the disciples argued about which of them was the greatest or whether they would have a share in Jesus' glory (10:35-45).

Sometimes the gospels salvage something of the early disciples' reputation, either by qualifying their faith as willing but fragile, or by omitting some more painful reminders about their inability to understand or follow Jesus' teaching. Matthew, for example, has the disciples respectfully approaching Jesus the Teacher with the question about greatness in the kingdom of heaven (Matthew 18:1-5) rather than arguing among themselves. Then, instead of portraying two of the Twelve, James and John, as ambitious for power, Matthew attributes the question about sharing in Jesus' glory to their mother (20:20-28). Likewise, Luke omits some of the more painful failures of the disciples, such as Mark's statement that they fled from the garden when Jesus was arrested (14:50). When finally Jesus is put to death, all four gospels make a point of saying that while many of the disciples fled when he was arrested, women who had accompanied him from Galilee witnessed his death, saw where he was buried, and set out to attend to his body at the tomb. They continued to remain faithful even after Jesus died and was buried. These women were the first witnesses to the resurrection.

Four Unique Portrayals of Women

Each of the Evangelists presents women and their roles differently. Put another way, with the focus on women, the uniqueness of each of the Evangelist's perspective can be seen. In Mark, the first gospel to be written (c. A.D. 65–70), women are blended into the background so that their significance might appear at first to be somewhat muted. Jesus encounters a few women along the way to Jerusalem—such as the daughter of Jairus (Mark 5:21-24, 35-43), the hemorrhaging woman (5:25-34), and the Syrophoenician woman who begs Jesus to cure her daughter (7:24-30). It may seem that women were not that important for Mark. However, near the end of his gospel, describing the arrest of Jesus, Mark notes this about the disciples: "All of them deserted him and fled" (14:50). Then in the very next chapter, at the crucifixion, he writes: "There were also women looking on from a distance" . . . who "used to follow him and provided for him when he was in Galilee; and there were many other women who had come up with him to Jerusalem" (15:40, 41). This description, in a nutshell, is the very definition of discipleship for Mark.

Matthew, who follows Mark in so many ways, might also appear to focus on other aspects of the gospel's effects on people rather than on the significance of women. For example, Matthew's infancy narrative focuses on Joseph rather than on Mary, as Luke does. But insertions of stories of women into Matthew's telling of the gospel are startling and very significant. For example, five women appear in Matthew's genealogy (Tamar, Rahab, Ruth, Bathsheba, and Mary). It is Matthew alone who includes an intervention on the part of Pilate's wife that he should have nothing to do with the execution of Jesus, an "innocent man" (27:19), indicating that the prophetic voice of women ought to be heeded. And in Matthew, the mother of James and John is important not only for her request for special favor for her sons but for her presence at the cross of Jesus.

Luke is sometimes considered to be sensitive to women's roles, but he has also been vilified for adding notations that appear to denigrate women. For example, the woman who anointed Jesus is known as "a sinner" (7:37), and women in Luke are sometimes corrected by Jesus. Without entering into that debate, we can point out that Luke includes more stories of women than any other Evangelist. For instance, three women have prominence in Luke's shaping of the infancy narrative (Mary, Elizabeth, and Anna in Luke 1–2). The poor widow in the Temple is praised by Jesus for offering her whole life in service to God (21:2-3), as contrasted with the leaders who "devour the widows' houses" just like her, and do so for their own enrichment and aggrandizement (20:45-47). Only Luke has the story of the daughter of Abraham, who having been cured by Jesus of her malady, "stood up straight and began praising God" (13:13). And only Luke tells of the widow of Nain whose son was raised by Jesus and restored to her (7:11-17). Luke alone pictures Jesus at home with Mary and Martha (10:38-42), and only Luke tells us that all along the way, prominent as well as ordinary women accompanied Jesus and the Twelve on his journey to Jerusalem and ministered to them (8:2-3).

John's Gospel further highlights the roles of women in Jesus' earthly ministry. The Samaritan woman, for example, engages Jesus in theological discourse and becomes one of the first missionaries of the gospel. Similarly, Jesus' mother presses him to perform his first miracle at Cana, one of the "signs" that reveals the meaning of Jesus' ministry and identity (2:1-11). John's Gospel also assigns significant companionship and dialogue roles to women as Jesus reveals his identity and mission. One way John develops his gospel story is through comparisons and contrasts. With regard to women, such contrasts are striking, sometimes startling. The Samaritan woman compares favorably to Nicodemus; the woman who anointed Jesus to Judas; Mary Magdalene to Peter himself. In the service of the gospel, such contrasts mean that women, no less than men, are called to hear and spread the word, to become witnesses of Jesus and of the gospel.

The Meaning for Us

Over forty years ago, Vatican II joined its authority with previous papal encyclicals encouraging Catholics to pursue Bible study and to use all the methods made available and accessible by contemporary biblical scholarship for a more fruitful understanding of the Scriptures. Communal rather than individual study and prayer has always characterized Catholic biblical study. Together we can encourage and challenge one another to see in the women we read about in the Scriptures our own stories and to follow their example with more courage and fidelity.

The gospels are not only about Jesus himself but about the women and men who believed that Jesus is the Messiah promised by God, and who transformed their lives so that the proclamation of Jesus' message of salvation would spread to the ends of the earth. The movement started by Jesus of Nazareth and his small following grew to become a great church despite persecution and the fears of its own messengers. People of every generation have read the gospels and found in them their own stories of conversion. Through the gospels we are called to leave behind our fears and doubts, our hesitations and obstacles, to become missionaries of the message of God's love for the world as revealed in Jesus.

It is remarkable that some of Jesus' highest praise is reserved for women who believe without seeing and trust without evidence. To the Canaanite woman, Jesus says, "Woman, great is your faith! Let it be done for you as you wish" (Matthew 15:28), and her daughter is immediately healed. Jesus tells the frightened and ill woman who dares to approach and touch him, "Daughter, your faith has made you well; go in peace, and be healed of your disease" (Mark 5:34). Jesus looks with compassion on his own mother and blesses her by commending her to the care of one he loves (John 19:27). Such stories are the stuff of the gospel, and they are there for us. It makes all the difference that they feature and hold up women who were hidden and overlooked in their society. Such women call us to come out of the shadows of our own timidity and fear, and take our responsible places among Jesus' disciples. The gospels call on men to treat women in a most respectful way, following the example of Jesus. The gospels call women to examine their Christian identity and reclaim the roles inherited from the courageous and faithful women in Jesus' life. The Evangelists show that the gospel requires the participation of all men and all women in the kingdom of God.

It is obvious that Jesus exemplifies and mandates justice for the downtrodden, inclusion for the outcasts, and mercy especially for those who have neither power nor rights of their own. Jesus is staunchly for the poor, the sick, sinners, and those his society consider outsiders. In the gospels these are represented in the stories about women and gentiles, and Jesus consistently turns his attention to people such as these and responds to their needs. We have to suspect that what is emphasized, time and again, by all four Evangelists is part of the revelation we are meant to learn from the gospel stories. Since we cannot account for Jesus' priorities from the culture and values of his time, it must be that they are an essential part of the new kingdom he proclaims as born among us believers.

In this Bible study, we will present six examples of women of the gospels and endeavor to identify potential lessons from their lives as described by the Evangelists. The stories of Anna and Elizabeth not only thrill and inspire us but also challenge us, like the good seed of the parable, to receive the word with "an honest and good heart, and bear fruit with patient endurance" (Luke 8:15). The women that followed Jesus from Galilee, including the mother of James and John, and persevered with him even to the cross and his burial, are models for us. Their watching and waiting prepared them for the resurrection and qualified them to proclaim it to others. Jesus' interactions with the Samaritan woman and Mary of Bethany led them to become true disciples and missionaries; they challenge us to do more to spread the gospel to all in need of hearing it.

Readers may be puzzled to discover that sessions on two of the most important women of the gospels are missing from this short study—Mary, the mother of Jesus, and Mary Magdalene. We are necessarily limited in our selection of which women to focus on, and we could not do justice to these very prominent disciples of Jesus. Extensive studies have been done on these two women named Mary, and we recommend that readers avail themselves of these resources.

Mary Ann Getty-Sullivan

Trusting in God

Luke 1:5-25, 39-45, 57-66

[1:5]In the days of King Herod of Judea, there was a priest named Zechariah, who belonged to the priestly order of Abijah. His wife was a descendant of Aaron, and her name was Elizabeth. [6]Both of them were righteous before God, living blamelessly according to all the commandments and regulations of the Lord. [7]But they had no children, because Elizabeth was barren, and both were getting on in years.

[8]Once when he was serving as priest before God and his section was on duty, [9]he was chosen by lot, according to the custom of the priesthood, to enter the sanctuary of the Lord and offer incense. [10]Now at the time of the incense offering, the whole assembly of the people was praying outside. [11]Then there appeared to him an angel of the Lord, standing at the right side of the altar of incense. [12]When Zechariah saw him, he was terrified; and fear overwhelmed him. [13]But the angel said to him, "Do not be afraid, Zechariah, for your prayer has been heard. Your wife Elizabeth will bear you a son, and you will name him John. [14]You will have joy and gladness, and many will rejoice at his birth, [15]for he will be great in the sight of the Lord. He must never drink wine or strong drink; even before his birth he will be filled with the Holy Spirit. [16]He will turn many of the people of Israel to the Lord their God. [17]With the spirit and power of Elijah he will go before him, to turn the hearts of parents to their children, and the disobedient to the wisdom of the righteous, to make ready a people prepared for the Lord." [18]Zechariah said to the angel, "How will I know that this is so? For I am an old man, and my wife is getting on in years." [19]The angel replied, "I am Gabriel. I stand in the presence of God, and I have been sent to speak to you and to bring you this good news. [20]But now, because you did not believe my words, which will be fulfilled in their time, you will become mute, unable to speak, until the day these things occur."

> Mary of Nazareth presents herself at the threshold of Elizabeth and Zechariah's house as the Mother of the Son of God. This is Elizabeth's joyful discovery: "The mother of my Lord comes to me!"
> —Pope John Paul II, *Redemptoris mater*, 13

²¹Meanwhile the people were waiting for Zechariah, and wondered at his delay in the sanctuary. ²²When he did come out, he could not speak to them, and they realized that he had seen a vision in the sanctuary. He kept motioning to them and remained unable to speak. ²³When his time of service was ended, he went to his home.

²⁴After those days his wife Elizabeth conceived, and for five months she remained in seclusion. She said, ²⁵"This is what the Lord has done for me when he looked favorably on me and took away the disgrace I have endured among my people." . . .

³⁹In those days Mary set out and went with haste to a Judean town in the hill country, ⁴⁰where she entered the house of Zechariah and greeted Elizabeth. ⁴¹When Elizabeth heard Mary's greeting, the child leaped in her womb. And Elizabeth was filled with the Holy Spirit ⁴²and exclaimed with a loud cry, "Blessed are you among women, and blessed is the fruit of your womb. ⁴³And why has this happened to me, that the mother of my Lord comes to me? ⁴⁴For as soon as I heard the sound of your greeting, the child in my womb leaped for joy. ⁴⁵And blessed is she who believed that there would be a fulfillment of what was spoken to her by the Lord." . . .

⁵⁷Now the time came for Elizabeth to give birth, and she bore a son. ⁵⁸Her neighbors and relatives heard that the Lord had shown his great mercy to her, and they rejoiced with her.

⁵⁹On the eighth day they came to circumcise the child, and they were going to name him Zechariah after his father. ⁶⁰But his mother said, "No; he is to be called John." ⁶¹They said to her, "None of your relatives has this name." ⁶²Then they began motioning to his father to find out what name he wanted to give him. ⁶³He asked for a writing tablet and wrote, "His name is John." And all of them were amazed. ⁶⁴Immediately his mouth was opened and his tongue freed, and he began to speak, praising God. ⁶⁵Fear came over all their neighbors, and all these things were talked about throughout the entire hill country of Judea. ⁶⁶All who heard them pondered them and said, "What then will this child become?" For, indeed, the hand of the Lord was with him.

Elizabeth was a woman of distinction, both because of her religious heritage and her own religious accomplishments. But it did not always seem so. Elizabeth and her husband, Zechariah, were both from the priestly line of Aaron, brother of Moses. "Both of them were righteous" (1:6), Luke tells us—the only time a woman is described as such in the New Testament. This means that Elizabeth, no less than her husband, was faithful and scrupulous in her observance of the Torah. Yet Elizabeth was disgraced (1:25) because she was barren, and her hopes for having a child were dimmed by her advanced age. Without a son, a woman of those times was desolate and pitiable. However, despite her situation, Elizabeth continued to do what she became noted for: She trusted God.

While Zechariah took his turn to offer sacrifice in the Temple, Elizabeth endured more of the silence that seemed to be the only response to her prayers. Time was running out. When her husband came out at last **Elizabeth was quick to believe.** from the sanctuary, mute and gesturing, Elizabeth must have wondered why God's answer to her would finally come in such a mysterious way. Like Eve, Elizabeth learned of the Lord's command from her husband, who had heard it more directly—Adam from the Lord, and Zechariah from the angel. But this time the woman would lead the way to fulfillment and grace. Elizabeth was quick to believe and exclaim, "This is what the Lord has done for me when he looked favorably on me and took away the disgrace I have endured among my people" (1:25).

In an appearance to Mary, the angel confirmed Elizabeth's prayer of praise, adding, "Nothing will be impossible with God" (1:37). Only Luke connects Mary and Elizabeth as kinswomen. Yet their pregnancies linked the women as no simple familial ties of flesh and blood could have done. Luke reinterprets family as based on common faith. Like Elizabeth, Mary saw her pregnancy as a sign of God working wonders in her life. Mary's response to God's message announced by the angel was one of generous hospitality to others: Mary hastened to join Elizabeth in grateful anticipation of the fulfillment of God's promises in their lives.

But more, both women proceed as prophets, that is, as people capable of interpreting God's will for themselves and others, and willing to act on it in their own lives. Mary "set out and went with haste" (1:39) to meet up with Elizabeth to celebrate their roles in God's plan. "With a loud cry," Elizabeth exclaims her faith in Mary's son, as she greets Mary as "mother of my Lord!" (1:42, 43). As if instructed by his mother, Elizabeth's child adds his own wordless echo, leaping for joy in recognition of the presence of the Lord among them. Her visit to Elizabeth is no mere act of human charity, for Mary withdraws just as Elizabeth is about to deliver her child, just when it would appear that Elizabeth would most need her kinswoman's physical and emotional support. Elizabeth and Mary's three-month visitation serves rather as a prophetic occasion to announce their solidarity with their sons for the salvation of all the world. They recognize the coming of the Messiah, and they rejoice because they have become instruments of God.

Elizabeth's child is born and named according to the angel's instruction to Zechariah, who must have somehow told Elizabeth, "He is to be called John" (1:60). Luke tells us no more of the satisfaction Elizabeth must have felt as all these things took place, even as she knew by faith that they would. Although Zechariah concludes the story of John's birth with a hymn of blessing, it is Elizabeth's strong and persevering faith that is conveyed. An awesome fear comes upon all the neighbors, who had previously doubted that Elizabeth's hopes would come to much or that she would conceive or that she was right in the naming of her son. Now they take the events that have happened through this woman to heart as they realize that "the hand of the Lord" (1:66) is with her as well as the child they must have thought she would never bear. And so, as the word spoken by the angel to Mary becomes flesh, Elizabeth recedes into the background, just as her son in turn will do when Jesus begins his own ministry.

Understand!

1. What are some of the ways Elizabeth takes a very active role in the shaping of this story?

   _____

   _____

   _____

   _____

   _____

   _____

2. Why do you think Luke indicates a kinship between Elizabeth and Mary and, by implication, between John and Jesus? (see 1:36). By what means does Luke suggest the more important roles for Mary and for Jesus?

   _____

   _____

   _____

   _____

   _____

   _____

3. Why does Luke describe the reaction of Elizabeth and Zechariah's neighbors and friends to the events? How do they add to the story? How do they show that these events are not just private between the two women but for everyone?

   _____

   _____

   _____

   _____

   _____

   _____

4. In what ways does Elizabeth act and speak prophetically in this passage? How will her words come to fulfillment later on?

_____

_____

_____

_____

_____

_____

5. List the various ways God communicates with people in this story. How does this compare with the way God communicates with Hannah in the story of the birth of the prophet Samuel (see 1 Samuel 1–2)? What other parallels between the two stories can you find?

_____

_____

_____

_____

_____

▶ In the Spotlight
The Problem of Barrenness

Elizabeth joins a rather prestigious line of Old Testament heroic mothers who suffered a shaky start because of their infertility: Sarah, Rachel, and Hannah, the mother of Samuel, to name a few. Considered as an anomaly of nature, barrenness was particularly problematic to a woman, because without children she actually had no future. It was also a cultural problem for the whole society, especially because religion was to be passed on from generation to generation. Ancient people had very little control over their world and felt themselves entirely dependent upon God and God's good will toward them in matters of life and death. Barrenness, like illness and even death itself, was considered a sign of God's "disapproval" that could only be removed by God. Medicine was suspect, a pagan work combining magic, herbs, and incantations to powerless and lifeless deities. The pious Israelite directed prayers to God in the face of an illness or a condition such as infertility, expressing humble submission to God's will. The miracle of God's intervention was all that could be hoped for, because the poor and truly needy—an apt description of the barren woman—had no other recourse but to God.

Grow!

1. Elizabeth appears to have felt disgrace because of her barrenness (see Luke 1:25). Have you ever felt disgrace by something that happened in your life, even if it wasn't your fault? How did faith in God help you overcome those feelings?

---

2. Elizabeth's prayer recognizes Mary as "blessed among women" (Luke 1:42). In what ways do you count yourself blessed? What blessedness do you celebrate, and how do you do that?

---

3. Elizabeth and Mary's visitation was a generous human response to their common situation and also a prophetic act of faith. Can you recall a situation in your life when a human act of kindness appeared to have meaning and significance for you beyond the actual act? What lasting effect did this have?

_____

_____

_____

_____

_____

_____

4. How is Elizabeth a model of strong and persevering faith? How did she exhibit trust in the Lord? How did she have the insight about Mary's impending pregnancy?

_____

_____

_____

_____

_____

_____

5. Elizabeth was a prophet—one who speaks on God's behalf and interprets events in the light of God's will. What situations in your life today call you to be a prophet? What obstacles, if any, prevent you from doing so?

_____

_____

_____

_____

_____

_____

▶ In the Spotlight
Scripture Celebrates God's Work in Our Lives

The example of Hannah (1 Samuel 1–2), with her copious tears and persistent prayer, illustrates the anguished cry of a woman desperate to conceive. But most important for us is Hannah's example of confidence and hope that God cared and would remedy her distress if asked. Similarly, Elizabeth is a woman of confidence and shows complete trust in God.

But it is Mary who turns the sentiments of Hannah and other Israelites into a model prayer for believers for all times. In her Magnificat (Luke 1:46-55), Mary sings of the reversals celebrated in God's kingdom: The mighty are thrown down and the lowly raised up, the rich are sent away empty and the hungry are given their fill. Mary gives voice to the amazement of the poor and the seemingly forgotten: God shows special tender care for them, attending to their every need and prayer. Elizabeth and Mary join their energies and their futures in unison, singing of all God has done for them and for countless others who, in their poverty and need, depend on God alone. In their encounter, we have an imitable example of how we can use the Scriptures to celebrate the works of God in our own lives. We join the company of men and women before us who lamented their loss and loneliness, expressed their hope in God, celebrated their faith and trust that God would take care of them, and praised God for allowing them to participate in the mystery of salvation.

Reflect!

1. Think about how you and your family or friends celebrate the birth of a child among you. What implications does this have for the family and community? What else can you do to express Christian hope and thanksgiving for the children of your family and church community?

2. The gospels offer believers a new way to think about children. Meditate on these words of Jesus to see how they change your own ideas:

> Then he took a little child and put it among them; and taking it in his arms, he said to them, "Whoever welcomes one such child in my name welcomes me, and whoever welcomes me welcomes not me but the one who sent me." (Mark 9:36-37)

> "Truly I tell you, unless you change and become like children, you will never enter the kingdom of heaven. . . . If any of you put a stumbling block before one of these little ones who believe in me, it would be better for you if a great millstone were fastened around your neck and you were drowned in the depth of the sea." (Matthew 18:3, 6)

> "Take care that you do not despise one of these little ones; for, I tell you, in heaven their angels continually see the face of my Father in heaven." (Matthew 18:10)

▶ In the Spotlight
A Pregnant Creation

Elizabeth comes to mind when we read Romans 8 in The Message, *a paraphrased version of the Bible by Eugene Peterson, in which St. Paul says the following:*

I don't think there's any comparison between the present hard times and the coming good times. . . . All around us we observe a pregnant creation. The difficult times of pain throughout the world are simply birth pangs. But it's not only around us; it's *within* us. The Spirit of God is arousing us within. We're also feeling the birth pangs. These sterile and barren bodies of ours are yearning for full deliverance. That is why waiting does not diminish us, any more than waiting diminishes a pregnant mother. We are enlarged in the waiting. We, of course, don't see what is enlarging us. But the longer we wait, the larger we become, and the more joyful our expectancy.
—Romans 8:18, 22-25, *The Message*

Act!

To prepare for what is to come in your life, place yourself consciously in the presence of God, and picture yourself pregnant with joyous expectation and trust. Say the Serenity Prayer slowly as you ask for serenity, courage, and wisdom, today and every day:

> God, grant me the serenity to accept the things
>   I cannot change,
> the courage to change the things I can,
> and the wisdom to know the difference.

▶ In the Spotlight
The Leap of Joy

An excerpt from The Reed of God, *by Caryll Houselander, a twentieth-century English Catholic writer:*

Many women, if they were expecting a child, would refuse to hurry over the hills on a visit of pure kindness. They would say they had a duty to themselves and to their unborn child which came before anything or anyone else.

The Mother of God considered no such thing. Elizabeth was going to have a child, too, and although Mary's own child was God, she could not forget Elizabeth's need—almost incredible to us, but characteristic of her.

She greeted her cousin Elizabeth, and at the sound of her voice, John quickened in his mother's womb and leapt for joy.

"I am come," said Christ, "that they may have life and may have it more abundantly." Even before He was born His presence gave life.

With what piercing shoots of joy does this story of Christ unfold! First the conception of a child in a child's heart, and then this first salutation, an infant leaping for joy in his mother's womb, knowing the hidden Christ and leaping into life.

How did Elizabeth herself know what had happened to Our Lady? What made her realize that this little cousin who was so familiar to her was the mother of her God?

She knew it by the child within herself, by the quickening into life which was a leap of joy.

If we practice this contemplation taught and shown to us by Our Lady, we will find that our experience is like hers.

If Christ is growing in us, if we are at peace, recollected, because we know that however insignificant our life seems to be, from it He is forming Himself; if we go with eager wills, "in haste," to wherever our circumstances compel us, because we believe that He desires to be in that place, we shall find that we are driven more and more to act on the impulse of His love.

And the answer we shall get from others to those impulses will be an awakening into life, or the leap into joy of the already wakened life within them.

—**Caryll Houselander,** *The Reed of God*

Watching
and
Waiting

Luke 2:22-38

2:22When the time came for their purification according to the law of Moses, they brought him up to Jerusalem to present him to the Lord 23(as it is written in the law of the Lord, "Every firstborn male shall be designated as holy to the Lord"), 24and they offered a sacrifice according to what is stated in the law of the Lord, "a pair of turtledoves or two young pigeons."

25Now there was a man in Jerusalem whose name was Simeon; this man was righteous and devout, looking forward to the consolation of Israel, and the Holy Spirit rested on him. 26It had been revealed to him by the Holy Spirit that he would not see death before he had seen the Lord's Messiah. 27Guided by the Spirit, Simeon came into the temple; and when the parents brought in the child Jesus, to do for him what was customary under the law, 28Simeon took him in his arms and praised God, saying,

> 29"Master, now you are dismissing your servant in peace,
>   according to your word;
> 30for my eyes have seen your salvation,
>   31which you have prepared in the presence of all peoples,
> 32a light for revelation to the Gentiles
>   and for glory to your people Israel."

33And the child's father and mother were amazed at what was being said about him. 34Then Simeon blessed them and said to his mother Mary, "This child is destined for the falling and the rising of many in Israel, and to be a sign that will be opposed 35so that the inner thoughts of many will be revealed—and a sword will pierce your own soul too."

> All who, like Simeon and Anna, persevere in piety and in the service of God, no matter how insignificant their lives seem in men's eyes, become instruments the Holy Spirit uses to make Christ known to others.
> —*The Navarre Bible: Saint Luke's Gospel*

[36]There was also a prophet, Anna the daughter of Phanuel, of the tribe of Asher. She was of a great age, having lived with her husband seven years after her marriage, [37]then as a widow to the age of eighty-four. She never left the temple but worshiped there with fasting and prayer night and day. [38]At that moment she came, and began to praise God and to speak about the child to all who were looking for the redemption of Jerusalem.

Anna lived a long life of waiting and hoping. She seems to have made a career of patience and trust. That's why she was able to recognize the Messiah, even when he came in the form of an infant, the son of a poor couple, Mary and Joseph. Luke elevates the ordinary to the sacred in the account of Anna the prophet, who upon seeing Jesus and before he was even able to do anything, announced to all awaiting the Redeemer that he had indeed come. Jesus, the One that would save Jerusalem and the world, had come, even as the faithful knew that he would.

Anna might have appeared to the world to have lived an unimportant life. People sometimes think of waiting as passive, an arms-folded boredom that idly passes the time until a good thing happens. That would not be a fitting description of Anna, who might better be compared to an expectant mother whose whole life is geared to what she is building and growing and preparing. Anna is a woman of all seasons. Probably married, as was the custom, at the onset of puberty, Anna's expectations of normal happiness were shattered early by the loss of her husband after only seven years. Without the eyes of faith, she might have been forgotten and relegated to complete obscurity.

> Anna's trust in God was active and tenacious.

But her trust in God was active and tenacious. She fostered her hopes with religious fervor, fasting and praying "night and day" (2:37). She persisted in believing in God, so that "at that moment" (1:38) when his parents arrived to present their son, Jesus, in the Temple, Anna was watching and waiting. Instantly she recognized Jesus as the Messiah, as if her whole life had been oriented to this meeting. Without hesitation she proclaimed his arrival as the fulfillment of all her own hopes and the expectations of all the other faithful in Jerusalem. Then she broke her silence, speaking "to all" (2:38) who, like her, trusted God's promises that the Messiah would come. When he did, Anna and the other faithful poor realized that their lives were changed forever and that their perseverance had paid off. They had been right to believe.

Luke's Gospel unfolds as a journey to Jerusalem. As preparation for this journey, Jesus himself retreats to Nazareth in Galilee. His journey will bring him back full circle to Jerusalem where it all started, as we learn from the story of Anna and the Presentation in the Temple. When he finally returns again as an adult confronting death, Jesus will enter Jerusalem and utter a prophet's lament over the city that failed to recognize the time of its visitation (Luke 19:41-44).

Yet no doubt some like Anna did recognize him and believe and bear witness of his identity to others. At the time of his passion, the "daughters of Jerusalem," for example, led a "great number" of mourners, Luke tells us, certainly recognizing in Jesus' condemnation and death an injustice that would cry out to heaven against the people and subject them all to God's judgment (Luke 23:27-31). Those women appear to have heeded Anna's prophecy about Jesus, and embraced her as their spiritual mother because it was she who first told of the promises fulfilled in Jesus with such excitement and faith. After his resurrection, Jesus commanded his followers to be his witnesses "beginning from Jerusalem" (24:47) and then to the "ends of the earth" (Acts 1:8). The story of the disciples' faithfulness to Jesus' command begins with Anna, the prophet who first announced Jesus' arrival in Jerusalem.

Anna is a symbol of active, vital vigilance that enabled her to instantaneously recognize Jesus as the Messiah and to persistently pass on this knowledge to others. Anna represents the whole of Israel as she awaits the redemption of God promised by the prophets. Like Israel, Anna, defenseless and poor, could do nothing to help herself. But she waited with faith and trust. Far from being passive, she readied herself with prayer and fasting. Her life of perseverance and hope was rewarded when at last Jesus appeared to her, and she knew it when the moment of God's revelation came. Though she did not know how, she believed the small babe presented by his poor parents in the Temple to be the Savior of the world.

Understand

1. How does Luke summarize Anna's religious background and credentials? Why do you think Luke includes these details? How are they important to the story?

_____

_____

_____

_____

_____

2. What features of discipleship does Luke use to describe Anna? How does that fit in with your own idea of discipleship?

_____

_____

_____

_____

_____

3. Luke builds much of his infancy narrative around portraits of three women: Elizabeth, Mary, and Anna. Whereas Elizabeth and Mary may appear to be essential figures and more intimately involved with Jesus, Anna's role is more general: She represents all of Israel. What does Anna's story add to your understanding of Jesus' infancy?

_____

_____

_____

_____

4. How was Anna active in preparing for and being able to recognize the time of God's "visitation" (Luke 19:44)? What hour of God's visitation should we be expecting in our own lives?

_____

_____

_____

_____

_____

_____

5. In explaining the parable of the sower (Luke 8:5-15), Jesus said that the seeds sown in good soil are those who hear God's word, receive it with an open and generous heart, and bring forth its fruit with perseverance. In your own words, how does Anna fulfill this description?

_____

_____

_____

_____

_____

_____

▶ In the Spotlight
Caring for Those Who Are Needy

In a patriarchal society, in which women belonged to men as chattel, widows represented the poor, the neglected, and the disenfranchised. Normally women could expect protection from fathers, husbands, and sons. But in their absence, the prophets demanded that the people and their leaders represent God in defending the defenseless. Widows and orphans are the primary examples of those who were most powerless. They also are living testimony that we humans are interdependent, that we need one another, and that we simply must take care of one another.

Today we have other social categories that replace the biblical image of the "widow," such as people with disabilities, the homeless, the unborn, and the dying. As believers we need to hear their cries for help, justice, and care, and assist them. Isaiah, speaking for God, says this in judgment against the people:

> When you stretch out your hands,
>   I will hide my eyes from you;
> even though you make many prayers,
>   I will not listen;
>   your hands are full of blood.
> Wash yourselves; make yourselves clean;
>   remove the evil of your doings
>   from before my eyes;
> cease to do evil,
>   learn to do good;
> seek justice,
>   rescue the oppressed,
> defend the orphan,
>   plead for the widow.
> (Isaiah 1:15-17)

But a little later, the prophet accuses the princes of the people for not listening to God. Isaiah says, "Your princes are rebels and companions of thieves. . . . / They do not defend the orphan, / and the widow's cause does not come before them" (1:23).

Jeremiah promises that even if all the other people are punished for their sins, orphans and widows will be spared, and their confidence in God will be vindicated. Jeremiah says, "Leave your orphans, I will keep them alive; / and let your widows trust in me" (49:11).

Grow!

1. In what active ways can a person show her expectations and longing, as well as her faith and confidence, that an anticipated event will happen? Have you ever waited a long time for an anticipated event to happen? How was your waiting "active"? How was it "passive"?

_____

_____

_____

_____

_____

_____

_____

2. What does vigilance mean in your spiritual life? What are we as Christians waiting for? What do we expect to see? Even if we are not literally in the Temple day and night, fasting and praying (Luke 2:37), what activities can we perform to show vigilance as we await the redemption promised to us?

_____

_____

_____

_____

_____

_____

_____

3. How is Anna a model of perseverance and a patron of those who have suffered loss or experienced great disappointment in life?

_____

_____

_____

_____

_____

_____

_____

4. Luke uses a "bracketing" technique by creating a parallel between Anna and a story near the end of Jesus' life of the widow who offers two small coins in the Temple of Jerusalem and is praised by Jesus for making an offering of "all she had"—her whole life (Luke 21:1-4). How does Anna, like that widow in Jerusalem, offer her whole life in the service of God? How can we offer our lives to God?

_____

_____

_____

_____

_____

_____

_____

5. Who in your life is a prophet who speaks to you of God and the things of God, and inspires you to live according to the gospel?

_____

_____

_____

_____

_____

_____

▶ In the Spotlight
Active Waiting

The late Dutch priest and author Fr. Henri Nouwen often spoke of a spirituality of waiting. These words are taken from a talk he gave on the topic:

Those who are waiting [in the Scriptures] are waiting very actively. They know that what they are waiting for is growing from the ground on which they are standing. That's the secret. The secret of waiting is the faith that the seed has been planted, that something has begun. Active waiting means to be present fully to the moment, in the conviction that something is happening. A waiting person is a patient person. The word "patience" means the willingness to stay where we are and live the situation out to the full in the belief that something hidden there will be manifest to us. Impatient people are always expecting the real thing to happen somewhere else and therefore want to go elsewhere. The moment is empty. But patient people dare to stay where they are. Patient living means to live actively in the present and wait there.

—**Henri Nouwen**, *The Spirituality of Waiting*

Reflect!

1. Meditate on the hidden life of Anna and examine its values. How is this a way of ministry you can identify with?

2. Reflect on the parallels among four widows of Luke's Gospel: Anna, the widow of Nain, the persistent widow of the parable, and the widow who gave two small copper coins. What do these

women have in common? How are they different? How do you think Jesus views them?

> Soon afterwards he went to a town called Nain, and his disciples and a large crowd went with him. As he approached the gate of the town, a man who had died was being carried out. He was his mother's only son, and she was a widow; and with her was a large crowd from the town. When the Lord saw her, he had compassion for her and said to her, "Do not weep." Then he came forward and touched the bier, and the bearers stood still. And he said, "Young man, I say to you, rise!" The dead man sat up and began to speak, and Jesus gave him to his mother. Fear seized all of them; and they glorified God, saying, "A great prophet has risen among us!" and "God has looked favorably on his people!" This word about him spread throughout Judea and all the surrounding country. (Luke 7:11-17)

> Then Jesus told them a parable about their need to pray always and not to lose heart. He said, "In a certain city there was a judge who neither feared God nor had respect for people. In that city there was a widow who kept coming to him and saying, 'Grant me justice against my opponent.' For a while he refused; but later he said to himself, 'Though I have no fear of God and no respect for anyone, yet because this widow keeps bothering me, I will grant her justice, so that she may not wear me out by continually coming.'" And the Lord said, "Listen to what the unjust judge says. And will not God grant justice to his chosen ones who cry to him day and night? Will he delay long in helping them? I tell you, he will quickly grant justice to them. And yet, when the Son of Man comes, will he find faith on earth?" (Luke 18:1-8)

He looked up and saw rich people putting their gifts into the treasury; he also saw a poor widow put in two small copper coins. He said, "Truly I tell you, this poor widow has put in more than all of them; for all of them have contributed out of their abundance, but she out of her poverty has put in all she had to live on." (Luke 21:1-4)

▶ In the Spotlight
The Value of Fasting

Anna spent her nights and days in prayer and fasting. Here is what Pope Benedict XVI says about the value and meaning of fasting:

We might wonder what value and meaning there is for us Christians in depriving ourselves of something that in itself is good and useful for our bodily sustenance. The Sacred Scriptures and the entire Christian tradition teach that fasting is a great help to avoid sin and all that leads to it. For this reason, the history of salvation is replete with occasions that invite fasting. . . .

In our own day, fasting seems to have lost something of its spiritual meaning, and has taken on, in a culture characterized by the search for material well-being, a therapeutic value for the care of one's body. Fasting certainly brings benefits to physical well-being, but for believers, it is, in the first place, a "therapy" to heal all that prevents them from conformity to the will of God. . . .

The faithful practice of fasting contributes, moreover, to conferring unity to the whole person, body and soul, helping to avoid sin and grow in intimacy with the Lord. . . . Denying material food, which nourishes our body, nurtures an interior disposition to listen to Christ and be fed by his saving word. Through fasting and praying, we allow him to come and satisfy the deepest hunger that we experience in the depths of our being: the hunger and thirst for God.

At the same time, fasting is an aid to open our eyes to the situation in which so many of our brothers and sisters live. In his first letter, St. John admonishes: "If anyone has the world's goods, and sees his brother in need, yet shuts up his bowels of compassion from him—how does the love of God abide in him?" (3:17). Voluntary fasting enables us to grow in the spirit of the Good Samaritan, who bends low and goes to the help of his suffering brother (*Deus Caritas Est*, 15). By freely embracing an act of self-denial for the sake of another, we make a statement that our brother or sister in need is not a stranger. . . .

From what I have said thus far, it seems abundantly clear that fasting represents an important ascetical practice, a spiritual arm to do battle against every possible disordered attachment to ourselves.

—**Pope Benedict XVI,** *Message for Lent 2009*

Act!

Reflect on this saying from Blessed Mother Teresa. How does it sums up the life of a disciple of Christ? How does it sum up your life? What is one specific action you could take this week to see one of these fruits in your life?

> The fruit of silence is prayer.
> The fruit of prayer is faith.
> The fruit of faith is love.
> The fruit of love is service.
> The fruit of service is peace.

▶ In the Spotlight
Simeon's Song

Anna wasn't the only one who saw Jesus in the Temple. Simeon was a "righteous and devout" man who had also been "looking forward to the consolation of Israel" (Luke 2:25). When he saw Jesus with Mary and Joseph, he took the baby in his arms and praised God. His prayer, known as the *Nunc Dimittis*, is the traditional gospel canticle of night prayer (also known as Compline) of the Church's Liturgy of the Hours. The title is formed from the opening words in the Latin: "*Nunc dimittis servum tuum, Domine*" ("Now thou dost dismiss thy servant, O Lord"). It is also often said by those retiring for the night:

> Lord, now you let your servant go in peace;
> Your word has been fulfilled.
> My eyes have seen the salvation
> You have prepared in the sight of every people,
> A light to reveal you to the nations and the glory of
> your people, Israel.

Ministering and Witnessing to Jesus

Mark 15:40-41, 47

15:40There were also women looking on from a distance; among them were Mary Magdalene, and Mary the mother of James the younger and of Joses, and Salome. 41These used to follow him and provided for him when he was in Galilee; and there were many other women who had come up with him to Jerusalem. . . .

47Mary Magdalene and Mary the mother of Joses saw where the body was laid.

> A disciple is, as the Lord himself taught us, whoever draws near to the Lord to follow him—to hear his words, to believe and obey him as king and doctor and teacher of truth.
> —St. Basil the Great, *On Baptism*, 1.2

Mark 16:1

16:1When the sabbath was over, Mary Magdalene, and Mary the mother of James, and Salome bought spices, so that they might go and anoint him.

Luke 8:1-3

8:1The twelve were with him, 2as well as some women who had been cured of evil spirits and infirmities: Mary, called Magdalene, from whom seven demons had gone out, 3and Joanna, the wife of Herod's steward Chuza, and Susanna, and many others, who provided for them out of their resources.

Luke 24:1-11

24:1But on the first day of the week, at early dawn, they came to the tomb, taking the spices that they had prepared. 2They found the stone rolled away from the tomb, 3but when they went in, they did not find the body. 4While they were perplexed about this, suddenly two men in dazzling clothes stood beside them. 5The women were terrified and bowed their faces to the ground, but the men said to them, "Why do you look for the living among the dead? He is not here, but has risen. [6]Remember how he told you, while he was still in Galilee, [7]that the Son of Man must be handed over to sinners, and be crucified, and on the third day rise again." [8]Then they remembered his words, [9]and returning from the tomb, they told all this to the eleven and to all the rest. [10]Now it was Mary Magdalene, Joanna, Mary the mother of James, and the other women with them who told this to the apostles. [11]But these words seemed to them an idle tale, and they did not believe them.

John 19:25

[19:25]Standing near the cross of Jesus were his mother, and his mother's sister, Mary the wife of Clopas, and Mary Magdalene.

In the Gospel of Mark, the first written notice that there were women who followed Jesus to Jerusalem actually appears near the end (15:40, 47; 16:1). Mark notes the presence of such women as silent witnesses to the death, burial, and resurrection of Jesus. However, Mark mentions women witnessing Jesus' teaching and miracles from the beginning of the gospel. For example, Jesus heals Peter's mother-in-law on the first busy day of miracles in Capernaum (1:30-31). And surely the woman with the issue of blood (5:25-34) and the parents of the young girl who was raised from the dead (5:21-24, 35-43) did not let Jesus simply fade out of their lives but "followed" him, at least in the figurative sense that he had permanently changed their lives. Also, the woman who anointed Jesus must have been one of his followers, since her prophetic act honored him and was done, Jesus said, in preparation for his burial (14:3-9).

The mention at the end of Mark's Gospel of women who had followed Jesus from Galilee to Jerusalem makes explicit an implication that runs like an undercurrent throughout this gospel: that is, despite the obstinate refusal to listen and even the rejection by many, some did hear and accept Jesus and follow him. By worldly standards these may have seemed like an insignificant few—the frightened and fickle Twelve, a smattering of lowly women, the odd bystander who took pity on Jesus and offered him wine on a sponge, or a lone centurion who only recognized Jesus when it seemed to be too late to matter. But Mark was writing for an audience almost overwhelmed by its own powerlessness and fear. They were challenged to identify with the vulnerable band that made up the first generation of disciples, and who made all the difference in spreading the message of Jesus and faith in his messiahship. And Mark's church would draw strength, encouragement, inspiration, and grace from the power of the example of lowly ones such as these, who formed the core of Jesus' first disciples.

The women at the cross, burial, and tomb of Jesus perform a number of functions that Mark associated with discipleship. They have followed Jesus despite hardship and suffering. They *listened* (Mark 4:3) as Jesus taught the people through parables and miracles, and repeatedly told his followers what was in store for him—and them. These women heard and integrated Jesus' predictions about the cross, so that when they came to pass, they were neither scandalized nor repulsed by it. Jesus' last word to his disciples before the passion was "*Watch!*" (13:37, RSV). His followers were to remain vigilant and *alert* (13:23), demonstrating their faithful awareness that what Jesus said would, in fact, take place. The women who followed Jesus *looked on* and witnessed (15:40) Jesus dying. They *saw* (16:4) that the stone had been rolled away where he had been buried. Their purpose in bringing spices to the tomb was to attend to Jesus' anointing (16:1) and thus *minister* to him one final time.

> The women at the cross, burial, and tomb . . . have followed Jesus despite hardship and suffering.

Luke does not name those who were present at Jesus' cross but refers to them simply as "the women who had followed him from Galilee" (23:49). Earlier, in the midst of the journey as Luke tells the story, the presence of women in Jesus' entourage and their contributions are expressly noted. Luke says in 8:2-3 that with Jesus were "some women who had been cured of evil spirits and infirmities: Mary, called Magdalene, from whom seven demons had gone out, and Joanna, the wife of Herod's steward Chuza, and Susanna, and many others who provided for them out of their resources." In saying this, Luke implies that these women, who had been cured of infirmities, followed Jesus and ministered to him and to others as a way of showing gratitude. Or perhaps Luke means that their discipleship is the result of experiencing Jesus' compassion. Their discipleship goes beyond the receiving of a simple cure, however, to actively participating in the mission of Jesus. Luke also suggests that the women who followed Jesus from Galilee to Jerusalem were respectable people of some means and that they were well-known by name in the Christian community. This information about such women is consistent with their indispensable support for the mission of the early church that Luke emphasizes in Acts (for example, Acts 1:14; 12:12-17; 16:1,13-14; 17:4, 12, 34).

The generosity of such women would have had a very dangerous dimension. Luke also makes a tantalizing suggestion in mentioning women with powerful connections, such as "Joanna, the wife of Herod's steward Chuza" (8:3). It is tempting to wonder if the news about Jesus, which must have spread around Herod's court, put such women as well as their husbands and families at risk. Women were supposed to remain at home, under the authority of their husbands. Thus, Herod's steward, a powerful man, would perhaps have been open to strong criticism and much worse because of his wife's activities ministering to Jesus. Other passages show how paranoid and cruel Herod and his family could be. If Herod feared whether Jesus was John raised from the dead (Luke 9:7-9), he probably would have been interested in interrogating members of his own court that knew Jesus. Herod would have been acting in character if he had threatened their lives, just as he so cruelly treated John the Baptist (Mark 6:14-29; Matthew 14:1-12).

There is no way to harmonize the names or identify further how many women followed Jesus to the cross and who they were. But it is noteworthy that across the spectrum of all four gospel accounts, women who had accompanied Jesus from Galilee were doing what disciples were supposed to do: following and being with Jesus, witnessing, ministering, and testifying to Jesus and to their faith in him.

Understand!

1. What would the presence of women among Jesus' entourage have added to Jesus' ministry? What did their presence say about Jesus?

   _____

   _____

   _____

   _____

   _____

   _____

2. According to Luke 8:1-3, the women who followed Jesus to Jerusalem and who supported him "out of their resources" had been "cured of evil spirits and infirmities." Why do you think Luke makes mention of this fact?

   _____

   _____

   _____

   _____

   _____

   _____

3. What do you think was in the minds of the women who followed Jesus to his death and came to his tomb? How does the presence of women at the end of Jesus' life deepen your understanding of their presence previously?

   _____

   _____

   _____

   _____

   _____

   _____

4. All four gospels convey the idea that the women who were present at the cross, burial, and tomb were disciples of Jesus. How are the women described at these events? What are they doing? Why? How did their actions reflect what Jesus taught about what it meant to follow him?

_____

_____

_____

_____

_____

_____

_____

5. Earlier John describes Jesus' mother as saying to the servants at a wedding feast in Cana, "Do whatever he tells you" (John 2:5). The next time John speaks of Jesus' mother, it is to say that she stood at the foot of the cross with some other women (19:25). What does this imply about her presence throughout Jesus' life? How does this observation deepen your appreciation of Mary's fidelity to Jesus and her own willingness to do whatever Jesus asked of her?

_____

_____

_____

_____

_____

_____

_____

▶ In the Spotlight
"To Follow" and "To Serve"

At the crucifixion, women are singled out as having been closely associated with Jesus and his movement even back in Galilee. Mark uses two verbs, "follow" and "serve," and he uses them in the continuous sense to express the role of women in Jesus' life. The use of the verb "follow" *(akolouthein)* suggests that the women can be called "disciples" of Jesus, since *akolouthein* is the usual Markan (and New Testament) word for discipleship. The word has this loaded meaning, for example, in Mark 6:1, where we are told, "He [Jesus] left that place and came to his hometown, and his disciples followed him."

The verb translated "serve" or "minister to" *(diakoneo)* also appears in the sense of "waiting on table" or "seeing to hospitality," as in the story of the cure of Peter's mother-in-law. After Jesus healed her, she immediately rose and ministered to him and his followers (Luke 4:39).

The women's ministry probably included tasks that constituted "women's work" in first-century Mediterranean society, such as washing clothes, preparing and cooking food, or carrying water. But some passages, like the explicit connection between following Jesus and ministering to him and the other disciples such as we find in Luke 8:2-3, suggest that prosperous and respectable women financially supported Jesus and his preaching ministry. The imperfect tense of the two verbs, "follow" and "minister to or provide for," indicates the women's repeated performance of their tasks while the group was in Galilee, during the journey to Jerusalem, and after Jesus' arrival in Jerusalem.

Grow!

1. What does it mean today to "watch" and "listen" to Jesus and his teaching? What implications does this have for your life? Do you need to make any changes?

_____

_____

_____

_____

_____

_____

_____

2. Women in Jesus' life followed him and ministered to him from Galilee to the empty tomb. Can you share some experiences of following Jesus when it seemed you were truly on a journey, covering new terrain, seeing different horizons, learning new things? What have been some of the milestones of discipleship in your own journey?

_____

_____

_____

_____

_____

_____

_____

3. Reflect on your journey of discipleship. What "miracle" launched you on the journey? How have you followed the crucified and risen Jesus? Where do you hope it will lead you?

_____

_____

_____

_____

_____

_____

_____

4. How is your appreciation of Mary affected by thinking of her not only as his mother but also as a disciple of Jesus? How can she be seen as a model of discipleship in your life?

_____

_____

_____

_____

_____

_____

5. For the women of the gospels, discipleship meant being a member of an entourage of others who are also called to "follow" Jesus. Why is it important for us to journey with other followers of Jesus? How has your relationships with other disciples of Christ enriched your faith life and journey?

_____

_____

_____

_____

_____

_____

▶ In the Spotlight
From the *Catechism of the Catholic Church*

Mary Magdalene and the holy women who came to finish anointing the body of Jesus, which had been buried in haste because the Sabbath began on the evening of Good Friday, were the first to encounter the Risen One. Thus the women were the first messengers of Christ's Resurrection for the apostles themselves. (641)

Christ's Resurrection cannot be interpreted as something outside the physical order, and it is impossible not to acknowledge it as an historical fact. It is clear from the facts that the disciples' faith was drastically put to the test by their master's Passion and death on the cross, which he had foretold [cf. Luke 22:31-32]. The shock provoked by the Passion was so great that at least some of the disciples did not at once believe in the news of the Resurrection. Far from showing us a community seized by a mystical exaltation, the Gospels present us with disciples demoralized ("looking sad" [Luke 24:17]) and frightened. For they had not believed the holy women returning from the tomb and had regarded their words as an "idle tale" [Luke 24:11]. When Jesus reveals himself to the Eleven on Easter evening, "he upbraided them for their unbelief and hardness of heart, because they had not believed those who saw him after he had risen" [Mark 16:14]. (643)

Reflect!

1. Jesus extends the invitation to follow him to all people—men, women, children, the poor, sinners, those with disabilities. Disciples of Jesus form a community called "church." Consider what it means to be part of the band of followers who, along

with many others, are called to follow Jesus all the way to the resurrection.

2. Meditate on the following Scripture passages about following Jesus:

> And looking at those who sat around him, [Jesus] said, "Here are my mother and my brothers! Whoever does the will of God is my brother and sister and mother." (Mark 3:34-35)

> "The Son of Man came not to be served but to serve, and to give his life a ransom for many." (Mark 10:45)

> "A disciple is not above the teacher, nor a slave above the master; it is enough for the disciple to be like the teacher, and the slave like the master. If they have called the master of the house Beelzebul, how much more will they malign those of his household!" (Matthew 10:24-25)

> Then [Jesus] said to them all, "If any want to become my followers, let them deny themselves and take up their cross daily and follow me." (Luke 9:23)

> As they were going along the road, someone said to him, "I will follow you wherever you go." And Jesus said to him, "Foxes have holes, and birds of the air have nests; but the Son of Man has nowhere to lay his head." (Luke (9:57-58)

▶ In the Spotlight
Mary Magdalene

Mary is identified in relation to her native village, Magdala, located near the Sea of Galilee, rather than in relation to a man, such as her father, husband, or son, as is the case with many women who appear in the gospels and was the custom of the times. This way of identifying her suggests that she was a single woman following Jesus out of her own conviction. Mark and Luke (compare Mark 16:9 and Luke 8:2) say that Jesus had expelled seven demons out of Mary. Her experience of being shown mercy and healing by Jesus was probably the basis for her single-minded commitment to him. Mary Magdalene is said to be present at the cross and at the burial, and is the first witness-messenger of the resurrection. No further description of this woman appears in the New Testament.

Mary Magdalene appears in all four of the gospels, and when mentioned, always appears first in a list of women followers of Jesus, except in John 19:25 where Jesus' own mother is identified first among those women at the foot of the cross. Although Mark and Luke note that Jesus healed her, there is no biblical connection between Mary of Magdala and the sinful woman said to have anointed Jesus (see Luke 7:36-50); there is even less reason to think of Mary as a former prostitute. In 591, the very popular and influential Pope Gregory I (c. 540–604) delivered a series of sermons about Mary Magdalene, linking her with the story of the unnamed "sinful woman" that anointed Jesus' feet out of gratitude and love (see Luke 7:36-50). In making that link, Gregory lent his authority and sanctioned previously circulating connections between accounts of separate episodes and different women in Luke. The link may simply have been due to the proximity of Luke's reference to Mary Magdalene out of whom Jesus "expelled seven demons" in 8:2-3 that follows the anointing story. Since all four gospels know of Mary

Magdalene, it does not seem reasonable that Luke would have omitted her name in telling the story of the anointing; Mark and Matthew say that the anointing took place in Bethany, and John identifies the woman who anointed Jesus as Mary of Bethany, not Mary of Magdala.

Act!

Read the "journey narrative" in the Gospel of Mark (8:22–10:52). Imagine yourself on the road to Jerusalem with Jesus. What are your sentiments as you listen to Jesus' instruction, observe your fellow companions, and hear Jesus talk about his death once you all reach the destination?

▶ In the Spotlight
Rabbis in Jesus' Time

The word "rabbi" means "my teacher." Students generally identified a certain rabbi and, perceiving him to be wise, offered to follow him. The student would devote himself to the rabbi and serve him while the rabbi discipled him. Rabbis were distinguished in part by the number and quality of the students they attracted. In the gospels we learn that Jesus took the initiative—that he chose his students and invited them to "follow" him. That invitation was open-ended and unconditional. It was also inclusive. Jesus welcomed men, women, and children. He ate with sinners and he healed the sick, Jews as well as Gentiles.

Sharing in
the Cross

Matthew 20:20-23

^{20:20}Then the mother of the sons of Zebedee came to [Jesus] with her sons, and kneeling before him, she asked a favor of him. ²¹And he said to her, "What do you want?" She said to him, "Declare that these two sons of mine will sit, one at your right hand and one at your left, in your kingdom." ²²But Jesus answered, "You do not know what you are asking. Are you able to drink the cup that I am about to drink?" They said to him, "We are able." ²³He said to them, "You will indeed drink my cup, but to sit at my right hand and at my left, this is not mine to grant, but it is for those for whom it has been prepared by my Father." (See also Mark 10:35-45.)

> Is it not an incontestable fact that women were the ones closest to Christ along the way of the cross and at the hour of his death?
> —**Pope John Paul II,** Homily, July 22, 2007

Matthew 27:55-56

^{27:55}Many women were also there, looking on from a distance; they had followed Jesus from Galilee and had provided for him. ⁵⁶Among them were Mary Magdalene, and Mary the mother of James and Joseph, and the mother of the sons of Zebedee.

There is an unnamed woman in the gospels remembered for transforming her concern for her sons into unconditional loyalty and devotion to Jesus. She makes only one request of Jesus, and it is only recorded by Matthew. But she has much to teach us because of what she herself learned.

Although Zebedee himself never appears in any of the gospels, at least he is named; his wife is known only as the mother of his sons. She exemplifies the way women were identified in Jesus' time—that is, they were known in relationship to their husbands and eventually, if all went well, to their sons. Undervalued for themselves, women gained some recognition through being "given" in marriage by their fathers or guardians, who arranged that their husbands would "take" them, usually with an exchange of some tangible value, a dowry. A woman's purpose was to bear children, preferably sons. And often women were identified, as this woman is, by the sons they bore. Even Mary, for example, is not named in John's Gospel, but is simply referred to as the "mother of Jesus" (John 2:1, 3, 5, 12; 19:25-27).

Yet the woman forever known as "the mother of the sons of Zebedee" (Matthew 20:20) exemplifies not only the way women were identified at the time of Jesus but the strikingly different way women are portrayed in the gospels. Matthew depicts her as a model of a disciple who might have started out following Jesus with mixed motives and aspirations. But then she pondered and came to accept Jesus' teaching about remaining with him in spite of suffering and persecution. And in the process, she was transformed into a real disciple. This woman is given special status in the Gospel of Matthew as a member of Jesus' entourage. She engages Jesus by asking for special treatment for her sons. Much more importantly, she demonstrates that she is a faithful and teachable disciple: Near the end of Matthew's Gospel, she is among those who witness Jesus' death. She must have heard about his command to testify to his resurrection (Matthew 28:19-20), and presumably, she did that too.

Matthew typically rescues Jesus' disciples from the somewhat harsh implications of some of Mark's descriptions of them. Matthew either softens the image or omits certain criticisms of Jesus' followers. For example, Mark frequently notes that the disciples did not understand Jesus or that they failed to believe him, especially when he predicted his passion (6:52; 9:32). According to Mark, when Jesus prophesied, for the third time, that he would go to Jerusalem and be put to death there, Zebedee's sons, James and John, irrelevantly and insensitively ask that they be given special authority in Jesus' kingdom (10:35-40). Later, when the rest of the Twelve hear about this request, they become indignant (10:41-45). Luke tells us that along the road to Jerusalem, the disciples argued about which one of them was the greatest, and that the argument continued even at the Last Supper (9:46; 22:24).

A Jewish mother's intervention for her children could be considered in the most understandable and benign way.

Only Matthew puts the request for special consideration in the mouth of James and John's mother (20:20-28; see also 18:1-2). Many interpreters explain this and other face-saving editorial changes that Matthew makes to his source, Mark, as attempts to uphold rather than degrade the status and authority of the Twelve. This may be a partial explanation of why Matthew has their mother make this request of Jesus, even though these two, with Peter, are among Jesus' most intimate associates. A Jewish mother's intervention for her children could be considered in the most understandable and benign way. From conception a mother should be involved in the promotion of her son's well-being. It may be said that the woman was only doing her duty.

But Matthew's real point in introducing James and John's mother is no doubt more theological than an observation of mere sociological interest. Matthew would not have been prone to favor stories of women. For example, he tells the annunciation and infancy story through the experience of Joseph and the dreams and visions that inspired him to take Mary as his wife and to protect her and the child, Jesus. The story is told, in fact, with hardly any mention of Mary (see Matthew 1–2). So it is remarkable that this same Matthew would highlight the intervention of the mother of two sons along the way to Jerusalem and note her presence at the end of Jesus' life. We may not be told her name, but thanks to Matthew, she is ever remembered for her fidelity as a follower of Jesus, even to the cross and tomb. We know that later her "sons of thunder" (Mark 3:17) also made good on their enthusiastic response when Jesus asked if they could drink the cup that he would drink (Matthew 20:22). But their mother apparently learned the depth of sacrifice involved in being a disciple of Jesus even before then.

Matthew's theological purpose in telling of the intervention of this woman is made clear by her second and third cameo appearances near the end of his gospel. She has been among Jesus' followers on his journey to Jerusalem. She has heard his teaching and seen his works. She asked for a favor and was undeterred by the apparent harshness of the demands implied in Jesus' answer. She kept following Jesus, watching and listening. She heard Jesus' prophecy about his passion, and she decided to undergo it with him. She is faithful, following Jesus not only when he is performing miracles or attracting crowds with the wisdom of his teaching. This woman, who is both wife and mother, is also and above all a disciple. She remains with Jesus as the story unfolds. She knows that his passion is also hers, his death shared by her, his resurrection a charge for her to tell her story to others.

Understand

1. What does the mother of James and John mean when she asks that her sons sit "one at your right hand and one at your left" (Matthew 20:21) when Jesus comes into his kingdom? What is Jesus' response?

   _____

   _____

   _____

   _____

   _____

   _____

2. What is James and John's reply? What is their mother's response, as shown by her actions later on? How does Matthew later depict this woman as a true disciple?

   _____

   _____

   _____

   _____

   _____

   _____

3. What does this episode say about Jesus' passion? What does it say about being a disciple of Jesus?

   _____

   _____

   _____

   _____

   _____

4. Why do you think that Jesus refers to the "cup" he is to drink? In which other episodes in his life does he refer to the "cup" he must drink?

_____

_____

_____

_____

_____

_____

5. What do you make of the indignation of the others to the request of James and John and their mother? Why do you suppose the gospels include the observation that the other ten apostles heard about the request and became indignant?

_____

_____

_____

_____

_____

_____

▶ In The Spotlight
Prophecy-Fulfillment Pattern in Matthew

Matthew is steeped in the Scriptures. More than any other Evangelist, Matthew often refers to or even cites specific Scripture passages showing how Jesus and events in his life fulfill the Old Testament prophecies. If Jesus makes a prediction or if some event calls for comment on Jesus' part, Matthew is sure to record that the prediction came to pass or that the event had some prophetic meaning.

The figure of the mother of Zebedee's sons is but one example of how this works. Matthew resolves the dilemma introduced by the woman's request of Jesus. Jesus predicts that she and her sons "will indeed drink my cup" (20:23), though he cautions that they do not know what they are asking. Nor do they know what is implied in their eager "We are able" (20:22). It is only at the cross that we learn that this woman must have pondered her own response and reconsidered the priorities of her request. Although her original question to Jesus was a natural one, she came to think and act on a different level of understanding of what Jesus' kingdom was all about. We don't hear about her again until she has followed Jesus to the cross and has begun to fulfill his prediction about "drinking" from the cup from which he was to drink. Her presence at the cross is an example of Matthew's use of the prophecy-fulfillment pattern and of her progress in the way of discipleship.

Grow!

1. What is your answer when Jesus asks you, "What do you want?" as he asked the mother of the sons of Zebedee (Matthew 20:21)? Did you ever want something that, in retrospect, you realized was not good for you? How did your thinking change?

_____

_____

_____

_____

_____

_____

2. Have your prayer requests for loved ones ever changed because of your relationship with Jesus? Explain.

_____

_____

_____

_____

_____

_____

3. When have you been tempted to intervene for your child? Can you recall a situation in which one of your parents intervened for you? In either case, what happened? Was it a wise decision? What did you learn from the situation?

_____

_____

_____

_____

_____

_____

4. Recall an occasion when you came to know some truth as a result of sticking with a person or situation, despite difficulty. How did patience and persistence pay off?

_____

_____

_____

_____

_____

_____

5. Have you ever replied, "I can!" only to find out that fulfilling that commitment was more difficult that you had imagined? Would it have been wiser (and therefore better) just to be silent? Did promising make you a better person?

_____

_____

_____

_____

_____

_____

_____

_____

▶ In The Spotlight
Another Mother in the Scriptures

Perhaps Matthew, who knew and loved the Scriptures, drew inspiration for his portrayal of this mother from a story very popular in Jesus' day of a mother and her seven sons at the time of the Maccabees, in the second century before Jesus. That story tells of the martyrdom of seven brothers, one by one, as their mother watches. Finally, the woman also is put to death (see 2 Maccabees 7). The family members are killed because they refuse to denounce their Jewish faith and heritage and succumb to the demands of Hellenistic tyrants. Adding to the drama and the heroism of this story, their tormentors demand that the mother instruct her sons to forsake their faith under penalty of torture and death. When they refuse, the tyrants make the mother watch as her sons are put to death. She speaks to each of them, from the eldest to the youngest, whose witness becomes the most haunting of all. But she does not encourage them to save themselves from death by abandoning God and their Jewish religious practices. Rather, she urges them to follow their faith and witness to God's fidelity by resisting the temptation to surrender.

The mother bears her own anguish and grief "with good courage because of her hope in the Lord" (2 Maccabees 7:20). In their native Hebrew not understood by their tormentors, she exhorts each of her children, saying,

> "I do not know how you came into being in my womb. It was not I who gave you life and breath, nor I who set in order the elements within each of you. Therefore the Creator of the world, who shaped the beginning of humankind and devised the origin of all things, will in his mercy give life and breath back to you again, since you now forget yourselves for the sake of his laws." (2 Maccabees 7:22-23)

Reflect!

1. Meditate on the place of the cross of Christ in your own life and spirituality. How has it helped you to better accept suffering— your own and that of your loved ones.

2. Reflect on these words of Jesus as you consider the crosses you may be carrying for him:

> "Blessed are those who are persecuted for righteousness' sake, for theirs is the kingdom of heaven. / Blessed are you when people revile you and persecute you and utter all kinds of evil against you falsely on my account. Rejoice and be glad, for your reward is great in heaven, for in the same way they persecuted the prophets who were before you." (Matthew 5:10-11)

"Whoever does not carry the cross and follow me cannot be my disciple." (Luke 14:27)

"Very truly, I tell you, unless a grain of wheat falls into the earth and dies, it remains just a single grain; but if it dies, it bears much fruit." (John 12:24)

▶ In The Spotlight
The Reality of the Cross

O strange and inconceivable thing! We did not really die, we were not really buried, we were not really crucified and raised again. Yet our imitation is only a symbol, though our salvation is in reality. Christ was actually crucified, and actually buried, and truly rose again; and all these things have been granted to us, that we may participate in his sufferings by imitation, and might gain salvation in reality.
—St. Cyril of Jerusalem

In all our actions, when we come in or go out, when we dress, when we wash, at our meals, before retiring to sleep, we make on our foreheads the Sign of the Cross. These practices are not committed by a formal law of Scripture, but tradition teaches them, custom confirms them, faith observes them.
—Tertullian

The cross is the unique sacrifice of Christ, the "one mediator between God and men" (1 Timothy 2:5). But because in his incarnate divine person he has in some way united himself to every man, "the possibility of being made partners, in a way known to God, in the paschal mystery" (*Gaudium et spes*, 22) is offered to all.
—*Catechism of the Catholic Church*, 618

Act!

Engage another person in a conversation about the relationship between personal ambitions, and suffering and persistence. Is suffering always a good thing? Ever a good thing? What role does it have in your own spiritual life? How does dialogue about suffering change your perception of the other person? How does it affect your own discipleship journey?

▶ In The Spotlight
A Mother's Persistence: St. Monica

St. Monica, mother of St. Augustine of Hippo, represents another instance of a mother's influence, persistence, and holy example. Augustine writes of her in his Confessions, *which he addresses to God. Here he tells of a dream she had that her son would eventually become Christian:*

My mother, your faithful one, wept to you on my behalf more than mothers are accustomed to weep for the bodily deaths of their children. For by the light of the faith and spirit that she received from you, she saw that I was dead. And you did hear her, O Lord, you did hear her and despised not her tears when, pouring down, they watered the earth under her eyes in every place where she prayed. You did truly hear her.

For what other source was there for that dream by which you consoled her . . . ? In her dream she saw herself standing on a sort of wooden rule, and saw a bright youth approaching her, joyous and smiling at her, while she was grieving and bowed down with sorrow. But when he inquired of her the cause of her sorrow and daily weeping (not to learn from her, but to teach her, as is customary in visions), and when she answered that it was my soul's doom she was lamenting, he bade her rest content and told her to look and see that where she was, there I was also. And when she looked she saw me standing near her on the same rule.

Where did this vision come from unless it was that your ears were inclined toward her heart? O Omnipotent Good, you care for every one of us as if you cared for him only, and so for all as if they were but one! . . .

By that dream, the joy that was to come to that pious woman so long after was predicted long before, as a consolation for her present anguish. Nearly nine years passed in which I wallowed in the mud of that deep pit and in the darkness of falsehood, striving often to rise, but being all the more heavily dashed down. But all that time this chaste, pious, and sober widow—such as you loved—was now more buoyed up with hope, though no less zealous in her weeping and mourning; and she did not cease to bewail my case before you, in all the hours of her supplication.

—St. Augustine, *Confessions,* Book III, Chapter XI

Eagerly
Spreading
the Gospel

John 4:7-30, 39-42

[4:7]A Samaritan woman came to draw water, and Jesus said to her, "Give me a drink." [8](His disciples had gone to the city to buy food.) [9]The Samaritan woman said to him, "How is it that you, a Jew, ask a drink of me, a woman of Samaria?" (Jews do not share things in common with Samaritans.) [10]Jesus answered her, "If you knew the gift of God, and who it is that is saying to you, 'Give me a drink,' you would have asked him, and he would have given you living water." [11]The woman said to him, "Sir, you have no bucket, and the well is deep. Where do you get that living water? [12]Are you greater than our ancestor Jacob, who gave us the well, and with his sons and his flocks drank from it?" [13]Jesus said to her, "Everyone who drinks of this water will be thirsty again, [14]but those who drink of the water that I will give them will never be thirsty. The water that I will give will become in them a spring of water gushing up to eternal life." [15]The woman said to him, "Sir, give me this water, so that I may never be thirsty or have to keep coming here to draw water."

[16]Jesus said to her, "Go, call your husband, and come back." [17]The woman answered him, "I have no husband." Jesus said to her, "You are right in saying, 'I have no husband'; [18]for you have had five husbands, and the one you have now is not your husband. What you have said is true!" [19]The woman said to him, "Sir, I see that you are a prophet. [20]Our ancestors worshiped on this mountain, but you say that the place where people must worship is in Jerusalem." [21]Jesus said to her, "Woman, believe me, the hour is coming when you will worship the Father neither

> Like the Samaritan woman, let us also open our hearts to listen trustingly to God's Word in order to encounter Jesus, who reveals his love to us and tells us: "I who speak to you am he" (John 4: 26), the Messiah, your Savior.
> —Pope Benedict XVI, Angelus Address, February 24, 2008

on this mountain nor in Jerusalem. ²²You worship what you do not know; we worship what we know, for salvation is from the Jews. ²³But the hour is coming, and is now here, when the true worshipers will worship the Father in spirit and truth, for the Father seeks such as these to worship him. ²⁴God is spirit, and those who worship him must worship in spirit and truth." ²⁵The woman said to him, "I know that Messiah is coming" (who is called Christ). "When he comes, he will proclaim all things to us." ²⁶Jesus said to her, "I am he, the one who is speaking to you."

²⁷Just then his disciples came. They were astonished that he was speaking with a woman, but no one said, "What do you want?" or, "Why are you speaking with her?" ²⁸Then the woman left her water jar and went back to the city. She said to the people, ²⁹"Come and see a man who told me everything I have ever done! He cannot be the Messiah, can he?" ³⁰They left the city and were on their way to him. . . .

³⁹Many Samaritans from that city believed in him because of the woman's testimony, "He told me everything I have ever done." ⁴⁰So when the Samaritans came to him, they asked him to stay with them; and he stayed there two days. ⁴¹And many more believed because of his word. ⁴²They said to the woman, "It is no longer because of what you said that we believe, for we have heard for ourselves, and we know that this is truly the Savior of the world."

John tells a story of an encounter between Jesus and a woman that is both attractive for its simplicity and intriguing for its eccentricities. It makes us wonder why John, who admits to being selective regarding the events he includes in his gospel (21:25), told this particular episode, especially since it seems to have no clear resolution or obvious purpose. Jesus is passing through a town and, encountering a woman at a well, asks for a drink and then proceeds to have a short discussion with her. Afterward she reports this encounter to others and invites them to come and decide for themselves who Jesus might be. What did John wish to convey with this story?

The context provides a partial answer to this question about John's intent. The story of the Samaritan woman appears after the account of Nicodemus' meeting with Jesus in chapter 3. Nicodemus provides an interesting contrast to the Samaritan woman. Nicodemus is an important leader of the Jews, a teacher of Israel. This unnamed woman is an outcast for a number of reasons: She is a foreigner, and worse, she is from Samaria, which had a long history of animosity with the Jews. She is not only a woman but one apparently shunned by her own townspeople for a morally reprehensible lifestyle that included five husbands.

Nicodemus comes to Jesus at night, seeking him out to ask a question about his identity. The woman arrives at Jacob's well at noon, the brightest hour of the day, and she is startled when Jesus speaks to her. She had come for a practical purpose: to draw water, not to question Jesus about theological matters or to debate his answers. Nicodemus appears to be left on the fence and in the dark. He is not ready to accept or understand Jesus' revelation. Nicodemus remains at the literal level of the dialogue with Jesus, confused about how a grown man can reenter his mother's womb and be born again (3:4). The woman begins at the literal level, identifying Jesus as he appears, as a Jew. But she shows that she is receptive to a deeper understanding of his identity, calling him a "prophet" (4:19), opening herself to the possibility that he is "greater than our ancestor Jacob" (4:12), and finally hearing Jesus' self-revelation, "I am he" (4:26)—the one, as the woman says, who will "proclaim all things to us" (4:25). She rushes to share her belief that Jesus is the Christ with others. And based on the word of Jesus, the Samaritans come to believe that Jesus is the "Savior of the world" (4:42).

John leaves open the enduring significance of Jesus' encounter both with Nicodemus and with the woman. But it seems as if the contrast John presents between the two would mean that the woman was much more ready to recognize Jesus, accept his revelation of himself, and spread the message to others than was Nicodemus.

Interpreters suggest we read this story of the Samaritan woman at the well in two parts: verses 7-15, about the woman's practical errand and her private encounter with Jesus; and verses 16-30, about the implications of this encounter for the mission of the gospel and for John's readers, including ourselves. In John 4:7-15 Jesus encounters the woman and asks for a favor. It may be significant that the cup of water he requests is the basis for Jesus' recognition of those who are "blessed of my Father" according to Matthew (see 10:42 and 25:34-35). John's Gospel is very interested in symbols such as water, food, and blood. It is the symbolic meaning of this encounter that dominates the second part of the story. The woman had come to the well seeking water to drink; she became interested in what Jesus had to say so that she would not have to continue to come to the well every day. Although Jesus initially asks her for a cup of water, he actually wishes to give her the gift of life-giving water. It is as if John forgets or simply drops the initial basis of this encounter, because he never does say whether Jesus received anything to drink or whether he drank from the cup the woman almost surely offered him.

The moment of the encounter, "about noon" (4:6), is significant. Women usually went in groups to draw water, and normally they did this either early morning or later in the day, after the heat of the sun had burned off. In the withering heat of noon, women were usually busy at home, cooking, taking care of the children, and performing other domestic duties. That the woman appears by herself suggests that she may have been reluctant to endure the comments of her peers or to risk being shunned by the other women because of her marital history and questionable morals.

John places a great deal of emphasis on community. When the woman first encounters Jesus, she is alone. She engages him in theological and spiritual dialogue, and she herself is transformed into a believer by her encounter. Then her personal "respond-ability" becomes social and communal. She cannot keep her experience and her faith to herself. She is compelled by joy to share it. She forgets the reason she initially went to the well. She leaves her water jug behind and rushes off to enthusiastically proclaim her experience to her neighbors and to invite them to "see" (4:29) for themselves.

> She cannot keep her experience and her faith to herself. She is compelled by joy to share it.

In the end it is possible to make a number of observations about the meaning and purpose of this story. John makes clear that people considered outcasts and insignificant, like the Samaritan woman, were frequently more receptive to the gospel than were many of Israel's leaders such as Nicodemus. Even the disciples were amazed that Jesus would engage in conversation with a woman. But Jesus seems not to linger a moment with this reservation. The woman, instantly upon recognizing Jesus, undertook the responsibility of telling others, echoing Jesus' own initial invitation to the first disciples,

"Come and see" (John 4:29; 1:39). The Samaritans receive the woman and her witness to her encounter with Jesus. As a result, they also come to believe. Samaritans and women become representative figures of eager acceptance of the gospel and its implications for transforming lives.

The new age begun by the coming of Jesus the Messiah means that the original grace exemplified in the equal status of men and women as the image of God can be expressed in their relationships. Jesus consistently elevates this woman's dignity—first, by asking something of her; then, by engaging her in theological discourse; and finally, by inviting her to bring others into the circle of faith. She is to be counted among Jesus' disciples and missionaries. Her being female and non-Jewish is no deterrent at all to her willingness, her ability, her worthiness, or her effectiveness as a minister of the gospel. Any bias against her is a product of the former age. On the basis of what Jesus has done for her, the townspeople hear her testimony and come to faith. They will believe, not only because of her, but because their own experience of Jesus has affirmed the truth.

Understand!

1. What are the progressive ways that the woman in this story recognizes and identifies Jesus?

_____

_____

_____

_____

_____

_____

_____

2. In John 4:9, where John speaks as a narrator, he says, "For Jews do not share things in common with Samaritans." What clues in this story help you to understand what beliefs Jews and Samaritans did share?

_____

_____

_____

_____

_____

_____

_____

_____

3. How did the woman's "disadvantages" become advantages to her?

_____

_____

_____

_____

_____

_____

4. How is this story more powerful because Jesus interacts with a woman and a Samaritan than if it were about an encounter with a man who was Jewish? What does this say about Jesus and the nature of discipleship?

_____

_____

_____

_____

_____

_____

_____

5. How is the woman representative of a true disciple of Jesus? Why do you think John includes this story so early in his gospel?

_____

_____

_____

_____

_____

_____

_____

_____

▶ In the Spotlight
Samaria and Acceptance of the Gospel

Luke supports the insinuation of John that the formerly intransigent and hostile Samaritans were among the first to accept the gospel. In a parable, Jesus portrays the Samaritan as the one who responds appropriately to the wounded traveler left to die by the side of the road by robbers (Luke 10:29-37). Luke also tells us that of the ten lepers cured, the single one to return to give thanks was the Samaritan (17:11-19). And in Acts, Luke notes that the mission of the disciples was very successful in Samaria, where many people received the gospel and great numbers were baptized (Acts 8:5-17).

Grow!

1. When have you ever been tempted to believe that some personal quality or attribute makes you ineligible to be a missionary for Christ? How does this story change your view of yourself and your usefulness in building God's kingdom?

_____

_____

_____

_____

_____

_____

_____

2. How might have the woman of the story been impeded if she had allowed self-consciousness to get in the way of her encounter with Jesus? Are you aware of any way that your own self-consciousness impedes your progress in spirituality?

_____

_____

_____

_____

_____

_____

_____

3. The woman of Samaria set out to perform a routine task, and her encounter with Jesus transformed her into an effective missionary. Can you think of an example from your own experience when openness to grace became an unsought opportunity to spread the gospel?

_____

_____

_____

_____

_____

_____

_____

4. Has anyone ever extended a "come and see" invitation to you about Jesus? If so, what were you invited to do? Think of ways you could extend such an invitation to others. Who would you invite? What would you invite them to do?

_____

_____

_____

_____

_____

_____

_____

5. How do you think about Jesus today as opposed to when you first encountered him? What do you know about Jesus now that you didn't know about him then?

_____

_____

_____

_____

_____

_____

▶ In the Spotlight
Representative Figures in John

From the story of the encounter between Jesus and the Samaritan woman, we can glean a number of insights, not only into Johannine theology, but also into the woman as representative of a disciple who spreads the good news she has seen and heard in Jesus. At the end of his account, John says, "There are also many other things that Jesus did; if every one of them were written down, I suppose that the world itself could not contain the books that would be written" (John 21:25; see 20:30-31). Yet John only recounts a limited number of miracles (he calls them "signs"), and he seems to tell them in an abbreviated way, concentrating instead on the controversies and dialogue they occasion and the interpretation they should be given. And some of the miracles John recounts, like changing water into wine, do not seem to be of the extraordinary caliber of those in the synoptic accounts, such as Jesus' healing of a group of lepers (Luke 17:11-19) or his exorcism of a man who had terrorized whole towns (Mark 5:1-20).

Sometimes John relates encounters that Jesus had with ordinary people, such as Nicodemus or the woman at the well, and we might even wonder why such stories, although interesting, survived and were incorporated into the gospel narrative. Readers of John are required to look beyond the literal meaning and see the fuller, often symbolic sense John is trying to convey. Many of the figures of John's Gospel are representative of various responses to Jesus. Readers are urged to ask themselves "Which character do I identify with?" and "What is my response to Jesus?" Am I like Nicodemus, the woman who came to the well for water, or the disciples who became distracted with the surprising identity of some of Jesus' choices of messengers?

Reflect!

1. Examine your religious and cultural prejudices. What common ground can you establish with people of other faith traditions? What can you do to open your own heart so that biases and prejudgments might not be an obstacle to spreading your joy and enthusiasm in your relationship with Christ?

2. Read and reflect on these passages in the Acts of the Apostles about other women disciples who did good works and spread the good news of God's love:

> On the sabbath day we went outside the gate by the river, where we supposed there was a place of prayer; and we sat down and spoke to the women who had gathered there. A certain woman named Lydia, a worshiper of God, was listening to us; she was from the city of Thyatira and a dealer in purple cloth. The Lord opened her heart to listen eagerly to what was said by Paul. When she and her household were baptized, she urged us, saying, "If you have judged me to be faithful to the Lord, come and stay at my home." And she prevailed upon us. (Acts 16:13-15)

> Now there came to Ephesus a Jew named Apollos, a native of Alexandria. He was an eloquent man, well-versed in the scriptures. He had been instructed in the Way of the Lord; and he spoke with burning enthusiasm and taught accurately the things concerning Jesus, though he knew only the baptism of John. He began to speak boldly in the synagogue; but when Priscilla and Aquila heard him, they took him aside and explained the Way of God to him more accurately. (Acts 18:24-26)

Now in Joppa there was a disciple whose name was Tabitha, which in Greek is Dorcas. She was devoted to good works and acts of charity. At that time she became ill and died. When they had washed her, they laid her in a room upstairs. Since Lydda was near Joppa, the disciples, who heard that Peter was there, sent two men to him with the request, "Please come to us without delay." So Peter got up and went with them; and when he arrived, they took him to the room upstairs. All the widows stood beside him, weeping and showing tunics and other clothing that Dorcas had made while she was with them. Peter put all of them outside, and then he knelt down and prayed. He turned to the body and said, "Tabitha, get up." Then she opened her eyes, and seeing Peter, she sat up. He gave her his hand and helped her up. Then calling the saints and widows, he showed her to be alive. This became known throughout Joppa, and many believed in the Lord. (Acts 9:36-42)

▶ In the Spotlight
From the *Catechism of the Catholic Church*

We know from the way Jesus related to women in the gospels that he saw them as persons with dignity who reflected the image of God. The Catechism *says that men and women are created in the image of God, perfectly equal and complementary:*

Man and woman have been *created*, which is to say, *willed* by God: on the one hand, in perfect equality as human persons; on the other, in their respective beings as man and woman. "Being man" or "being woman" is a reality which is good and willed by God: man and woman possess an inalienable dignity which comes to them immediately from God their Creator [cf. Genesis 2:7, 22]. Man and woman are both with one and the same dignity "in the image of God." In their "being-man" and "being-woman," they reflect the Creator's wisdom and goodness. (369)

Men and women were made "for each other"—not that God left them half-made and incomplete: he created them to be a communion of persons, in which each can be "helpmate" to the other, for they are equal as persons ("bone of my bones . . .") and complementary as masculine and feminine. (372)

Act!

Resolve to learn and pray about religious prejudices in our world. Ask questions of an acquaintance of another religious tradition or denomination about what they believe and why. Try to find common ground concerning your beliefs and motivations. Identify three areas of commonality, if possible.

▶ In the Spotlight
The Surprises of God

The Benedictines have a custom, derived from the *Rule of Saint Benedict*, that even the youngest member of the community ought to be listened to because the Spirit blows where it will; wisdom can be found in the most unexpected places. And through stories like the woman of Samaria, in which an unprepared, uneducated, and surprisingly unlikely person became a vehicle for spreading the gospel, Christians throughout the centuries have been assured that the work of the Holy Spirit is alive and strong.

Surely one of the best examples of the surprises of God is found in the example of Mother Teresa of Calcutta. Beginning from when she was a young girl in Macedonia, she overcame language barriers, timidity, poverty, frailty, and a myriad of other obstacles to become a giant missionary and to begin a work that will long survive.

Born in Skopie in 1910, Agnes Gonxha Bojaxhiu joined the Sisters of Loreto in Dublin in 1928 and was sent to India, where she taught in a Calcultta high school. She left the order to found the Missionaries of Charity, through which her service to the poorest of the poor spread around the world. After her death in 1997, the process for her sainthood was quickly begun, and she was beatified in 2003.

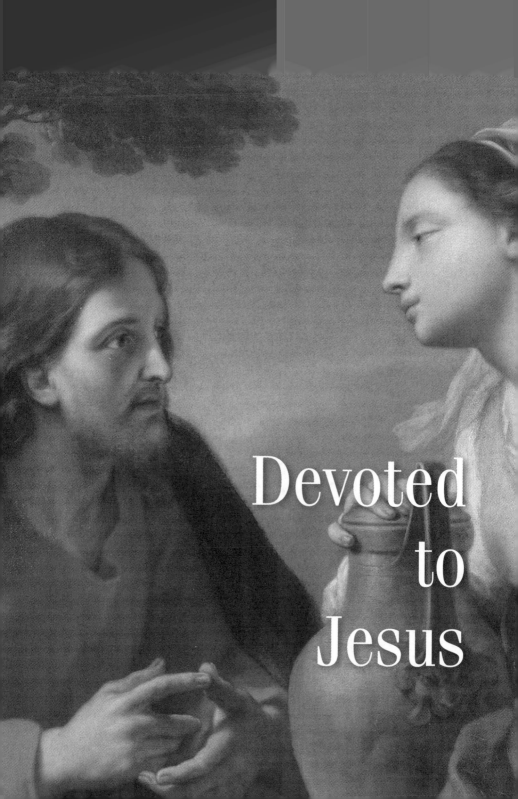

Devoted
to
Jesus

Luke 10:38-42

10:38Now as they went on their way, he entered a certain village, where a woman named Martha welcomed him into her home. 39She had a sister named Mary, who sat at the Lord's feet and listened to what he was saying. 40But Martha was distracted by her many tasks; so she came to him and asked, "Lord, do you not care that my sister has left me to do all the work by myself? Tell her then to help me." 41But the Lord answered her, "Martha, Martha, you are worried and distracted by many things; 42there is need of only one thing. Mary has chosen the better part, which will not be taken away from her."

> Mary not only wants to hear the word; by listening she wants to receive the Lord into herself, she wants to be his vessel.
> —Adrienne von Speyr, *Three Women and the Lord*

John 11:28-45

11:28[Martha] called her sister Mary, and told her privately, "The Teacher is here and is calling for you." 29And when she heard it, she got up quickly and went to him. 30Now Jesus had not yet come to the village, but was still at the place where Martha had met him. 31The Jews who were with her in the house, consoling her, saw Mary get up quickly and go out. They followed her because they thought that she was going to the tomb to weep there. 32When Mary came where Jesus was and saw him, she knelt at his feet and said to him, "Lord, if you had been here, my brother would not have died." 33When Jesus saw her weeping, and the Jews who came with her also weeping, he was greatly disturbed in spirit and deeply moved. 34He said, "Where have you laid him?" They said to him, "Lord, come and see." 35Jesus began to weep. 36So the Jews said, "See how he loved him!" 37But some of them said, "Could not he who opened the eyes of the blind man have kept this man from dying?"

³⁸Then Jesus, again greatly disturbed, came to the tomb. It was a cave, and a stone was lying against it. ³⁹Jesus said, "Take away the stone." Martha, the sister of the dead man, said to him, "Lord, already there is a stench because he has been dead four days." ⁴⁰Jesus said to her, "Did I not tell you that if you believed, you would see the glory of God?" ⁴¹So they took away the stone. And Jesus looked upward and said, "Father, I thank you for having heard me. ⁴²I knew that you always hear me, but I have said this for the sake of the crowd standing here, so that they may believe that you sent me." ⁴³When he had said this, he cried with a loud voice, "Lazarus, come out!" ⁴⁴The dead man came out, his hands and feet bound with strips of cloth, and his face wrapped in a cloth. Jesus said to them, "Unbind him, and let him go." ⁴⁵Many of the Jews therefore, who had come with Mary and had seen what Jesus did, believed in him.

John 12:1-8

¹²:¹Six days before the Passover Jesus came to Bethany, the home of Lazarus, whom he had raised from the dead. ²There they gave a dinner for him. Martha served, and Lazarus was one of those at the table with him. ³Mary took a pound of costly perfume made of pure nard, anointed Jesus' feet, and wiped them with her hair. The house was filled with the fragrance of the perfume. ⁴But Judas Iscariot, one of his disciples (the one who was about to betray him), said, ⁵"Why was this perfume not sold for three hundred denarii and the money given to the poor?" ⁶(He said this not because he cared about the poor, but because he was a thief; he kept the common purse and used to steal what was put into it.) ⁷Jesus said, "Leave her alone. She bought it so that she might keep it for the day of my burial. ⁸You always have the poor with you, but you do not always have me."

There is sparse enough material about Mary of Bethany in the gospels, and the little the Evangelists tell us is often confused with stories of other women and Jesus. We are indebted to Luke and John for what we do know of this woman. Most of it describes her actions, which express her devotion to Jesus. She is a woman of few words. We hear about an exchange between Martha and Jesus about Mary in Luke 10:38-42. A story of Jesus' encounter with Mary after the death of her brother, Lazarus, appears in John 11:28-45. Then, after Jesus raises Lazarus, they dine in Bethany, and Mary anoints Jesus' feet with costly ointment (12:1-8). These three vignettes featuring Mary of Bethany provide rich insights into the diverse roles of women in the early church.

Luke 10:38-42 appears in the context of Jesus' journey to Jerusalem, a theme especially emphasized by Luke in 9:5–19:28. Jesus is followed by his disciples on a long journey to Jerusalem, where he will be put to death. In the course of this journey, Jesus is often featured dining with his disciples and others, engaged in conversation with them, and teaching them. Sometimes his companions ask him questions and at other times they challenge him, especially about his associations with people like tax collectors and sinners, women, and people with illnesses and disabilities. Whether walking along the road or reclining at table, Jesus often assumes the role of leader or host as he instructs his followers on the high cost, the dangers, and the rewards of discipleship. This is the general context of the short exchange between Jesus and Martha over Mary's behavior. This incident can be understood as an instruction about the appropriate role of a sister-disciple of Jesus.

Mary herself appears to have a passive role in the story. She is the object of Martha's complaint to Jesus. Bethany is not mentioned. We only know that Mary, Martha, and Lazarus lived in Bethany from the Gospel of John. Luke might have neglected to mention Bethany because it is a village only about two miles from Jerusalem, and he places this incident at Martha and Mary's home early in Jesus' journey, long before he reaches the city where he will die. In Luke's perspective, the location of this conversation is not important here. Luke is developing various lessons and insights about the nature, demands, and priorities of discipleship as he paints a picture of Jesus making his way to Jerusalem.

The brief exchange between Martha and Jesus over Mary's role in the household was probably meant to enlighten the Lukan community about the appropriate role of women in the house churches that provided the context for the believers' worship, reflection on social issues, and instruction to new converts. Martha complained that Mary ought to be assisting her at table rather than sitting at Jesus' feet listening to his teaching. Luke suggests that Martha's complaint derived from the fact that she was "distracted with much serving (*diakoneo*)" (10:40, RSV). Jesus' answer affirms Mary's choice while chiding Martha for being "worried and distracted by many things" while "there is need of only one thing" (10:42). It seems that Martha must learn to prioritize her own choices and come to accept them or change them. Clearly, Jesus is not downgrading duties of hospitality, since in the next chapter we will hear him tell the story of the Good Samaritan, which is all about taking care of others. But Jesus refuses to side with those who would limit women's choices to the single role of "serving at table" rather than hearing, contemplating, and spreading the word of the gospel.

In chapters 11 and 12 of John's Gospel, there is a portrait of Mary of Bethany painted from another angle. The focus of the story in John 11 is on Lazarus, and to some extent, his sister Martha. Yet Mary's role is also important. That Jesus often visited his friends there is implied. Jesus loved Lazarus and his sisters, yet he postponed going to them, even when he heard that Lazarus was ill. Martha's close relationship with Jesus is implied in her complaint when he finally does come. "Lord, if you had been here, my brother would not have died" (11:21).

Remarkably, while Martha went out immediately to greet Jesus, Mary "stayed at home" (John 11:20). It is as if John echoes Luke's portrayal of Mary as quietly contemplating the meaning of events. After a brief conversation with Jesus, Martha returns to the house and informs her sister, "The Teacher is here and is calling for you" (11:28). Twice John remarks that Mary got up quickly (11:29, 31). After Mary repeats the words of Martha, Jesus asks where they had laid Lazarus, and the Jews mourning with Mary respond, "Come and see" (11:34). These words are the same that Jesus himself had used at the beginning of John's Gospel to the followers of John the Baptist (1:39). They are echoed by the Samaritan woman calling for the townspeople to discover their own faith in Jesus (4:29). And with similar words, Jesus invites Thomas to validate his faith in the resurrection (20:27).

The gospel could hardly pay a higher tribute to this woman nor memorialize her in a more appropriate way.

When Mary weeps, Jesus is also overcome with emotion and weeps, too, at the loss of his friend Lazarus. We may also think of Mary Magdalene weeping at the tomb (John 20:11). The tears of Mary of Bethany, Jesus, and Mary of Magdala illustrate the reality of death. But they also indicate that for believers, death is not the final word. When Jesus calls out to Lazarus, he comes forward, unbound, set free from death.

We next hear about Mary in the following chapter of John's Gospel, six days before the Passover that will coincide with Jesus' own death. In the intervening days, Jesus appears to move back and forth between Bethany and Jerusalem, perhaps using the house of his three friends in Bethany as his base as he prepares for the feast. Lazarus and his sisters "gave a dinner" at which Martha served and Lazarus was with Jesus at table. Ordinarily, men ate together while women, children, and slaves ate separately. Mary took costly ointment and anointed

Jesus' feet with it and wiped them with her hair, filling the house with the ointment's fragrance as she did so. Mary penetrated a boundary that would have excluded her. Judas' protest that the ointment could have been sold and the money given to the poor is met with Jesus' defense of Mary's action. Jesus says that she has done this for his burial, adding, "You always have the poor with you, but you do not always have me" (12:8). The anointing of Jesus by Mary is not interpreted as an act of gratitude for restoring Lazarus or a merely a mark of hospitality. Jesus is insinuating that Mary's action is prophetic. She recognizes him as the Bridegroom who is to come. She cannot help but celebrate.

According to John, Jesus himself follows Mary's example, and on the night before he died, he washes the feet of his disciple-friends, as Mary of Bethany had done in her wholehearted service of him. The gospel could hardly pay a higher tribute to this woman nor memorialize her in a more appropriate way. Mary of Bethany learned that Jesus had come "not to be served but to serve, and to give his life [as] a ransom for many" (Mark 10:45). Mary exemplifies one who chose the better part, the one thing necessary. She is a prophet remembered for her acts of generous and fearless devotion and her witness to Jesus. And her memory opens up a world of possibilities to both women and men disciples of Jesus. Mary of Bethany invites us to "come and see" and, finally, believe and serve, offering up our lives in love and in the spread of the gospel.

Understand!

1. What clues are in the text to suggest that Jesus was a good friend of Mary, Martha, and Lazarus? How do you think their friendship with Jesus affected the way Martha and Mary spoke to him?

   _____

   _____

   _____

   _____

   _____

2. What is the significance of Jesus' response to Martha's complaint? What is the "better part" (Luke 10:42) that will not be taken from Mary?

   _____

   _____

   _____

   _____

   _____

3. In Jesus' day women had clearly defined roles and did not speak with men when they were out in public. Even within the household, they did not mix with men. How do both Luke and John portray Mary of Bethany as breaking though cultural boundaries that restricted women?

   _____

   _____

   _____

   _____

   _____

4. Why do you think Jesus did not go to Bethany sooner, thus healing Lazarus and sparing Mary and Martha their grief? How do Martha and Mary express their grief differently?

_____

_____

_____

_____

_____

_____

5. According to John 12, what is the motivation for Mary's anointing of Jesus? Why does Judas protest and why, according to John, is his protest insincere? Why is it also inappropriate?

_____

_____

_____

_____

_____

_____

▶ In the Spotlight
The Meal Setting in the Gospels

Many of Jesus' miracles as well as the lessons he teaches occur in people's homes. So, for example, Jesus in the early days of his ministry enters Peter's home and cures his mother-in-law, who "immediately . . . got up and began to serve them" (Luke 4:39). After Jesus invites Levi to follow him, Luke says that the former tax collector "gave a great banquet for him in his house" (5:29). Jesus also dines in the home of a Pharisee (14:1), and there he takes on the role of the host, observing how the guests jockey for seats of honor and advocating instead that his disciples choose the lowest places (14:7-11), even inviting the "poor, the crippled, the lame, and the blind" to a banquet (14:13). Jesus' teaching upends the status quo and offers an alternative lifestyle consistent with the values of the kingdom of heaven. For Luke, criteria for behavior in the Christian community are based not on social etiquette or norms but on justice according to the reign of God. That Jesus' instruction is often presented in private homes suggests that the community of disciples who gathered in house churches recalled the words and example of Jesus to help them proceed along the Way he had shown them, in the direction he had pointed out, drawing on the values he had accentuated as he himself walked toward Jerusalem.

The meal setting also suggests that the early Christian communities understood the Eucharist as the perfect place to work out issues that arose in the community, such as the appropriate use of money and goods and the importance of honest leadership. As host of the Eucharistic meal, which was known as the "Lord's Supper," Jesus is the authority whose word and example keep the community on the course of true discipleship.

Grow!

1. Mary of Bethany's actions in these episodes spoke louder than words. Have you ever been challenged by the actions of others to change your own? How can the story of Mary of Bethany guide you in your own search for holiness and devotion to Jesus?

_____

_____

_____

_____

_____

_____

2. In what ways does Mary of Bethany present a picture of a strong personality that ought to be remembered by the early Christians and by us? What qualities of Mary can we emulate in our own lives?

_____

_____

_____

_____

_____

_____

3. How do you react to Jesus' weeping at the tomb of Lazarus? What does it say about Jesus? How can this image comfort you in your own sorrow?

_____

_____

_____

_____

_____

_____

4. The early church used the household as the basic model for the new society of equals created by the disciples of Jesus. Instruction was given during meals. Participants were referred to as "brothers and sisters." What values are consistent with this setting? In what ways can you use your own home to build the body of Christ and to form disciples?

_____

_____

_____

_____

_____

_____

5. The Church may be considered the household of Christ. Here believers can form alternative communities that don't have to follow the dictates of the larger society. What essential and unique qualities characterize leaders and fellow members of Christ's household? Which of these characteristics do you most want to grow in, and why?

_____

_____

_____

_____

_____

_____

▶ In the Spotlight
The Engaging Spirit of Mary of Bethany

The three portraits of Mary of Bethany presented to us by Luke and John show us a very free woman, wrapped in peace and generosity, and enthusiastic about expressing her single-minded devotion to Jesus. She appears not to care much about the criticism of others—not her sister, who insinuates that she is lazy and inconsiderate; not those at table, who think that her grief is expressed inappropriately; and not Judas, who says that her extravagance is wasteful and ought to be stopped.

These same qualities can be detected in the images of several modern-day saints. In his delightful book *My Life with the Saints* (Loyola Press, 2006), author James Martin says he was first drawn to Dorothy Day by a snapshot of her. Immediately upon seeing her, he wanted to follow her, because she looked as if she knew where she was going. In a similar way, Martin continues, the subtle smile in a photo of Thérèse of Lisieux suggests she is privy to a wonderful secret. In yet another example, Martin says that a photo of Mother Mary Joseph Rogers, the founder of the

Maryknoll sisters, captures the spirit of the distinctive spirituality of Maryknoll: "expansive, welcoming, confident" (209-211). These three saints could form a composite of Mary of Bethany. You would want to accompany her and to be her friend.

Reflect!

1. Compare John's account of the anointing of Jesus with the accounts of Mark (14:3-9) and Matthew (26:6-13) of this action by an unnamed woman. What are some similarities and differences? Can you think of reasons this story would have survived and been told by the early Christians, even if it was used in a number of different ways?

2. Mary's anointing of Jesus with the expensive ointment was an act of extreme generosity. Meditate on the following Scripture passages in which Jesus depict acts of generosity. How do these passages reflect the heart of God? How do they reflect your own heart?

> "For this reason the kingdom of heaven may be compared to a king who wished to settle accounts with his slaves. When he began the reckoning, one who owed him ten thousand talents was brought to him; and, as he could not pay, his lord ordered him to be sold, together with his wife and children and all his possessions, and payment to be made. So the slave fell on his knees before him, saying, 'Have patience with me, and I will pay you everything.' And out of pity for him, the lord of that slave released him and forgave him the debt." (Matthew 18:23-27)

> "For the kingdom of heaven is like a landowner who went out early in the morning to hire laborers for his vineyard. After agreeing with the laborers for the usual

daily wage, he sent them into his vineyard. When he went out about nine o'clock, he saw others standing idle in the marketplace; and he said to them, 'You also go into the vineyard, and I will pay you whatever is right.' So they went. When he went out again about noon and about three o'clock, he did the same. And about five o'clock he went out and found others standing around; and he said to them, 'Why are you standing here idle all day?' They said to him, 'Because no one has hired us.' He said to them, 'You also go into the vineyard.' When evening came, the owner of the vineyard said to his manager, 'Call the laborers and give them their pay, beginning with the last and then going to the first.' When those hired about five o'clock came, each of them received the usual daily wage. Now when the first came, they thought they would receive more; but each of them also received the usual daily wage. And when they received it, they grumbled against the landowner, saying, 'These last worked only one hour, and you have made them equal to us who have borne the burden of the day and the scorching heat.' But he replied to one of them, 'Friend, I am doing you no wrong; did you not agree with me for the usual daily wage? Take what belongs to you and go; I choose to give to this last the same as I give to you. Am I not allowed to do what I choose with what belongs to me? Or are you envious because I am generous?' So the last will be first, and the first will be last." (Matthew 20:1-16)

"A man was going down from Jerusalem to Jericho, and fell into the hands of robbers, who stripped him, beat him, and went away, leaving him half dead. Now by chance a priest was going down that road; and when he saw him, he passed by on the other side. So likewise a

Levite, when he came to the place and saw him, passed by on the other side. But a Samaritan while traveling came near him; and when he saw him, he was moved with pity. He went to him and bandaged his wounds, having poured oil and wine on them. Then he put him on his own animal, brought him to an inn, and took care of him. The next day he took out two denarii, gave them to the innkeeper, and said, 'Take care of him; and when I come back, I will repay you whatever more you spend.' Which of these three, do you think, was a neighbor to the man who fell into the hands of the robbers?" He said, "The one who showed him mercy." Jesus said to him, "Go and do likewise." (Luke 10:30-37)

▶ In the Spotlight
Wisdom from the Church Fathers

Mary's "better part" will be realized in its fullness in heaven, according to this sermon by St. Augustine:

You, Martha, if I may say so, are blessed for your good service, and for your labors you seek the reward of peace. Now you are much occupied in nourishing the body, admittedly a holy one. But when you come to the heavenly homeland, will you find a traveler to welcome, someone hungry to feed, or thirsty to whom you may give drink, someone ill whom you could visit, or quarrelling whom you could reconcile, or dead whom you could bury?

No, there will be none of these tasks there. What you will find there is what Mary chose. There we shall not feed others, we ourselves shall be fed. Thus what Mary chose in this life will be realized there in all its fullness; she was gathering fragments from that rich banquet, the Word of God. Do you not wish to know what we will have there? The Lord himself

tells us when he says of his servants, "Amen, I say to you, he will make them recline and passing he will serve them."
—St. Augustine of Hippo

Act!

Actions often speak louder than words, as Mary's gesture of anointing Jesus' feet shows us. This week convey love, devotion, and respect toward some member of your family, your relatives, or your social circle who might need the affirmation. Do this not by words but by a meaningful gesture or act.

▶ In the Spotlight
Praise for the Faith of Martha and Mary

These Christian Orthodox hymns celebrate the faith of both Martha and Mary:

You fervently believed in Christ and His marvelous acts,
O Martha and Mary, sisters of Lazarus.
You were adorned with radiant virtues
and were found worthy to be numbered with the saints;
together with holy Lazarus pray to God for us.

Since ye believed in Christ with strong and ardent faith,
and ever worshipped His divine and mighty deeds,
ye both adorned yourselves with all the splendor
of sacred virtues.
With your holy brother now,
ye are also vouchsafed to dwell with the ranks of Saints on high,
O ye sisters of Lazarus;
and with him, O wise Mary and Martha,

ye pray for us all unto the Master.

In the town of Bethany, ye dwelt of old;
now in Heaven ye abide in Paradise,
where our Lord's countenance shineth.
For ye gave your hearts and souls up with fervent longing
unto Him that is the Life and the Resurrection;
as ye stand on high, O Mary and Martha,
pray Him to grant salvation to us.

Practical Pointers for Bible Discussion Groups

A Bible discussion group is another key that can help us unlock God's word. Participating in a discussion or study group—whether through a parish, a prayer group, or a neighborhood—offers us the opportunity to grow not only in our love for God's word but also in our love for one another. We don't have to be trained Scripture scholars to benefit from discussing and studying the Bible together. Bible study groups provide environments in which we can worship and pray together, and strengthen our relationships with other Christians. The following guidelines can help a group get started and run smoothly.

Getting Started

- Decide on a regular time and place to meet. Meeting on a regular basis allows the group to maintain continuity without losing momentum from the previous discussion.

- Set a time limit for each session. An hour and a half is a reasonable length of time in which to have a rewarding discussion on the material contained in each of the sessions in this guide. However, the group may find that a longer time is even more advantageous. If it is necessary to limit the meeting to an hour, select sections of the material that are of greatest interest to the group.

- Designate a moderator or facilitator to lead the discussions and keep the meetings on schedule. This person's role is to help preserve good group dynamics by keeping the discussion on track. He or she should help ensure that no one monopolizes the session and that each person—including the shyest or quietest individual—is offered an opportunity to speak. The group may want to ask members to take turns moderating the sessions.

• Provide enough copies of the study guide for each member of the group, and ask everyone to bring a Bible to the meetings. Each session's Scripture text and related passages for reflection are printed in full in the guides, but you will find that a Bible is helpful for looking up other passages and cross-references. The translation provided in this guide is the New Revised Standard Version (Catholic Edition). You may also want to refer to other translations—for example, the New American Bible or the New Jerusalem Bible—to gain additional insights into the text.

• Try to stay faithful to your commitment, and attend as many sessions as possible. Not only does regular participation provide coherence and consistency to the group discussions, but it also demonstrates that members value one another and are committed to sharing their lives with one another.

Session Dynamics

• Read the material for each session in advance, and take time to consider the questions and your answers to them. The single most important key to any successful Bible study is having everyone prepared to participate.

• As a courtesy to all members of your group, try to begin and end each session on schedule. Being prompt respects the other commitments of the members and allows enough time for discussion. If the group still has more to discuss at the end of the allotted time, consider continuing the discussion at the next meeting.

- Open the sessions with prayer. A different person could have the responsibility of leading the opening prayer at each session. The prayer could be a spontaneous one, a traditional prayer such as the Our Father, or one that relates to the topic of that particular meeting. The members of the group might also want to begin some of the meetings with a song or hymn. Whatever you choose, ask the Holy Spirit to guide your discussion and study of the Scripture text presented in that session.

- Contribute actively to the discussion. Let the members of the group get to know you, but try to stick to the topic so that you won't divert the discussion from its purpose. And resist the temptation to monopolize the conversation, so that everyone will have an opportunity to learn from one another.

- Listen attentively to everyone in the group. Show respect for the other members and their contributions. Encourage, support, and affirm them as they share. Remember that many questions have more than one answer and that the experience of everyone in the group can be enriched by considering a variety of viewpoints.

- If you disagree with someone's observation or answer to a question, do so gently and respectfully, in a way that shows that you value the person who made the comment, and then explain your own point of view. For example, rather than saying, "You're wrong!" or "That's ridiculous!" try something like "I think I see what you're getting at, but I think that Jesus was saying something different in this passage." Be careful to avoid sounding aggressive or argumentative. Then watch to see how the subsequent discussion unfolds. Who knows? You may come away with a new and deeper perspective.

- Don't be afraid of pauses and reflective moments of silence during the session. People may need some time to think about a question before putting their thoughts into words.

- Maintain and respect confidentiality within the group. Safeguard the privacy and dignity of each member by not repeating what has been shared during the discussion session unless you have been given permission to do so. That way everyone will get the greatest benefit out of the group by feeling comfortable enough to share on a deep and personal level.

- End the session with prayer. Thank God for what you have learned through the discussion, and ask him to help you integrate it into your life.

- The Lord blesses all our efforts to come closer to him. As you spend time preparing for and meeting with your small group, be confident in the knowledge that Christ will fill you with wisdom, insight, grace, and the ability to see him at work in your daily life.

Sources and Acknowledgments

Session 1: Elizabeth

Page 19
John Paul II, *Redemptoris mater,* accessed at http://www. vatican.va/holy_father/john_paul_ii/encyclicals/documents/ hf_jp-ii_enc_25031987_redemptoris-mater_en.html.

Page 29
Eugene Peterson, *The Message: The Bible in Contemporary Language* (Navpress Publishing Group, 2002), 319.

Page 31
Caryll Houseland, *The Reed of God* (Notre Dame, IN: Christian Classics, an imprint of Ave Maria Press, 2006), 61, www.avemariapress.com.

Session 2: Anna

Page 33
The Navarre Bible: Saint Luke's Gospel, with a commentary by the members of the Faculty of Theology of the University of Navarre (Dublin, Ireland: Four Courts Press, 1993), 60.

Page 42
Henri Nouwen, *The Spirituality of Waiting,* taken from an article condensed from a tape available from Ave Maria Press. Accessed on the Web at http://www.ciu.edu/resources/ displaypdf.php?25.

Page 45

Pope Benedict XVI, *Message for Lent 2009*, accessed at http://www.vatican.va/holy_father/benedict_xvi/messages/ lent/documents/hf_ben-xvi_mes_20081211_lent-2009_ en.html. Copyright © 2009 Libreria Editrice Vaticana. Used with permission.

Session 3: The Women Who Followed Jesus from Galilee

Page 49

Basil the Great, *On Baptism*, 1.2, quoted in *God's Word Today*, Vol. 31, No. 10 (October 2009), 26.

Session 4: The Mother of the Sons of Zebedee

Page 65

John Paul II, Homily, July 22, 2007, accessed at http:// oldarchive.godspy.com/meditations/Mary-has-chosen-the-better-part-and-it-will-not-be-taken-from-her-Meditation-by-Pope-John-Paul-II.cfm.html.

Page 75

Quotations from Tertullian and Cyril of Jerusalem taken from *The Way of the Fathers: Praying with the Early Christians* by Mike Aquilina (Huntingdon, IN: Our Sunday Visitor, 2000), 48 and 49.

Page 77

Adapted from *Confessions*, St. Augustine, Book III, Chapter XI, accessed at http://www.ccel.org/ccel/augustine/confess .iv.xi.html.

Session 5: The Samaritan Woman

Page 79
Benedict XVI, Angelus Address, February 24, 2008, accessed at http://www.vatican.va/holy_father/benedict_xvi/ angelus/2008/documents/hf_ben-xvi_ang_20080224_en.html.

Session 6: Mary of Bethany

Page 95
Adrienne von Speyr, *Three Women and the Lord* (San Francisco: Ignatius Press, 1986), 86.

Page 109
Sermon by St. Augustine taken from Sermon 103, 1-2, 6: PL 38, 613, 615 for the Feast of Saint Martha, sister of Mary and Lazarus, on July 29. Accessed at http://www. crossroadsinitiative.com/library_article/161/Martha_and_ Mary____St._Augustine.html.

Page 109
Orthodox Hymns taken from Mary of Bethany, Orthodox Wiki, accessed at http://orthodoxwiki.org/Mary_of_Bethany.

The Word Among Us
Keys to the Bible Series
For Individuals or Groups

T hese studies open up the meaning of the Scriptures while placing each passage within the context of the Bible and Church tradition.

Each of the six sessions features

- The Scripture text to be studied and insightful commentary
- Questions for reflection, discussion, and personal application
- "In the Spotlight" sections that offer wisdom from the saints, personal testimony, and fascinating historical background

Here are just a few of our popular titles:

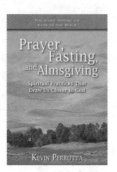
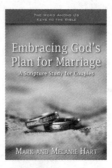
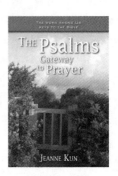

Treasures Uncovered: The Parables of Jesus

Praying, Fasting, Almsgiving

Embracing God's Plan for Marriage

The Psalms: Gateway to Prayer

Check out all the studies available in this series
by going online at **bookstore.wau.org**
or
call Customer Service at **1-800-775-9673**